GET

Pat O'Driscoll

1

Getting Hard! - © Copyright 2012 by Chauffour
Books

Published by Chauffour Books

1st Print edition 2.01 – May 2012

www.chauffourbooks.co.uk

Amazon ISBN: 978-1477516522

Also available in ebook on Amazon Kindle

Introduction

A long time ago, I was misguided enough to work for a local council. It was a sad day, not for me but for all those poor institutionalised bastards who padded in to work so safe, both in their anonymity and job security, that life posed them no challenges - until I turned up.

Somewhere on that plain, I met a man beside me who was desperate to do a little better. Don't get me wrong, he was never going to shine, nor even rise, but maybe he might get a little more of his just dues by applying a tiny bit more effort and a lot of hope. Possibly, that man was nicknamed Try Hard.

In his head was another council, one that discussed things in such a democratic format that often its meetings went on for hours, or even days, before eventually reaching an un-dramatic, disappointing and usually wrong outcome.

They say a Camel is really a Horse that was designed by a committee.

Maybe that same committee designed Milton Keynes?

1

'But I don't have any euros!' protested Try to the thin-faced woman behind the glass window, frantically waving the ten pound note in front of her impressive moustache.

'Cinq euros! Five!' she demanded, ignoring the note.

For a fourth time he tried, raising his voice and talking slowly, over-exaggerating every word. Behind him a car horn blared, then another behind that.

'Noooo, euuuurrrrooooss!'

Try had had some euros of course; he was a man who planned things with military precision. Like all good soldiers, Try kept his euros in his money belt and he kept that strapped around his middle. Well, usually he did. But the car ferry had spanned a tedious three hours and, not unexpectedly, Try had spent most of that time throwing up in the grossly unhygienic toilets, as they rocked back and forward, slamming the doors of the empty cubicles with alarming regularity, often on his fingers. In a gallant attempt not to fill his new money belt with vomit, Try had removed it and hung it on the door handle. That was the last he saw of it. While his head was stuck down the lavvy, an athletic looking man in a brown leather jacket and woollen beanie hat had pushed open the door, its lock long broken, to check he was OK. Try nodded that 'what the sodding hell did it look like?' and the man had left him in peace. In peace but, as he later discovered, penniless!

'It's Eeenglish moneeey, you stupid frog!' yelling louder as all English people do when trying to communicate with foreigners. 'It is used all over the woooorrrllllddddd'

'Well not eeerrrre, eeett eees not!' was the only reply that rather the masculine woman could offer.

Eyeing the red flimsy barrier in front of him, the more adventurous side of Try's brain considered driving the Skoda through it and tearing off down the auto-route, periodically hiding out in burnt-out barns to avoid the police helicopters. His mind reconsidered this as a man appeared in front of him with a machine-gun and he nearly shat himself! The gun was the biggest thing he had seen outside of Star Wars IV - the Empire strikes matches, or whatever the subtitle was - and it was pointing directly at his head through the semi-tinted windscreen of his new car. Why, oh why, hadn't he ordered the bullet-proof glass option, he thought, contemplating on whether to get out and run or mow the gendarme down where he stood. The gun got bigger as it came closer, poking in through his open window, gripped tightly by leather gloves. Try tried to shut the window, fumbling with the switch. It wouldn't go up. Instead the passenger side window went down.

'Allez avec moi?' said the owner of the gloved hands and the murderous looking weapon. Try counted to three and attempted to get out of the car, no mean feat when you are parked 6 inches from a concrete bollard on which stands a blue smoked-glass kiosk, which in turn houses a rather smug-looking French woman who could have doubled for Freddie Mercury.

Looking pityingly at him, the gendarme made a driving motion with his hands, gun now back on his shoulder. Try started the car as the barrier raised. Try stalled the car.

In his head, part of his brain said: *'Why hadn't he opted for the automatic transmission? Or possibly that Hummer he had seen in GQ magazine? Only a hundred grand, well worth it in times like these?'* but then he wondered if a Hummer would actually fit through the narrow gap between the pay kiosks.

Maybe not?

Then his tired and somewhat overactive mind imagined himself effortlessly sliding the gear-leaver of his Hum-Vee vehicle, full military specification, and reversing over the cars in the queue behind him, crushing their little heads as they honked on their stupid horns. Possibly some of their eyes would pop out with a dramatic squelch, splattering on the windscreens or even out onto the tarmac for the seagulls to eat. Try's tired mind often thought like this.

On the third attempt at starting the engine, the car shuddered forwards a little too fast, catching the officer on the back of the leg. Eyes narrowing behind aviator sunglasses, the moustachioed gendarme slowly raised his sub-machine gun once again, with his gloved finger itching on the trigger. Try was quite glad the window was open as a rather unhealthy odour arose from the seat beneath him while he made a gallant attempt to follow the blue-suited officer in first gear, not too closely, towards a lay-by full of men dressed in leather.

'Trevor Richard Yashati Hard,' repeated Try for the third time. 'My mother was Albanian,' he added by way of further explanation. 'Tee-Arrrgghh-Why-HARD.'

Moustaches were common place in the forces, possibly compulsory, but these guys had taken the letter of the law into their own hands. The part of his brain that dealt with such matters considered that such a fine array of bristles would make an exceptional display in the window of that old brush shop in Bloxwich, as the man in front of him tried to read his writing. 'People call me Try. Try Hard. Don't you see, it is an English joke? My mother liked the English humour, quite a few Albanians do apparently.' They didn't see. Humour to them was about as rare as hen's teeth, which was another common myth, as he was well aware. Try had caught a hen once and it had nearly bitten his finger off, sure proof that hen's did in fact have teeth.

Or was it a goose?

'Well, Monsieur 'AARD, if you cannot pay, you cannot use. Would I try and use your Eeenglish roads without paying? Non. Would I visit your 'ouse and take you duug, without paying? Non. Would I...'

'Alright, alright,' he sighed, getting the message. They wouldn't accept his money and there was no bank nearby. 'Can I go now?' He was tempted to add: 'before I have to sweep the entire motorway with your fine facial hair,' but decided against it.

Not being the best at three point turns, Try didn't intend to knock the motor-cycle over, it was just parked badly. Ignoring the fist waving gendarme in his rear view mirror, he manoeuvred the Skoda round and out on to the side road. Oh well, it would be a long slow trek down to La Rochelle without using the auto-route, even with the radio on. Beside him, his mobile phone sounded the French National Anthem, something he had downloaded on his last day back in the office.

'Trevor Hard,' he shouted, balancing the phone on his shoulder as he tried to change gear and steer the car at the same time. 'No thank you. No. Oh. No problem. Yes, and you. Bye!' Closing the phone, Try glanced up at his red face in the mirror. OK, that had definitely been one of his bigger mistakes, putting the advert in the singles column in the Droitwich Gazette. He had thought it sounded quite attractive.

HARD. WAITING FOR YOU!

That was all it had said; a simple sentence, followed by his mobile number. As the newspaper had charged by the word, keeping the message short had saved him money. Try never thought to check which section it had gone into, and that had possibly been a minor oversight. Since that fateful day, nearly 4 weeks ago, he had had dozens upon dozens of calls from men with deep voices, all wanting to meet up, usually somewhere private.

Try wasn't gay, at least he didn't think he was.

No, he definitely wasn't.

Driving down the side road, he tried to imagine beautiful girls, all dancing, with him, naked. Girls. A man with a swirling moustache smiled pleasantly at him as he passed and Try's blood pulsed again. Girls, he was only interested in girls. That was why he was in France, for some Cherchez la femme! In his best Sean Connery voice, Try used his killer chat up line.

'I'm Hard!' holding his hand out in an imaginary handshake. He only ever did this with women; men tended to get all defensive and immediately wanted a fight. Except the gay ones, who would probably give him a knowing smile; that is if he knew any, which he didn't.

Well apart from that guy who served in the canteen, Helen had said he may be that way, but she had no proof.

In fact he had only ever tried it on one woman. Unsurprisingly, she had slapped him. Helen had told him that women didn't like that sort of thing, especially women who work for Droitwich town council. Helen Cartwright knew a thing or two about women, although she had never been married herself. But, she had said, those French women...well, they loved all that, she had seen a documentary on it. They liked to be sweet-talked by an English Gentlemen, she had said, while he sipped his half pint of shandy in the Briar Rose club one Thursday lunchtime. That very afternoon, Try had been booking his next holiday and Helen had suggested France was a good place for a pick-up, especially down in the South-West by the sea. That was where he was heading now.

*

Less than a mile behind him, Baxter Collins had the Skoda in his sights. Baxter was quite excited as he drove his blue Ford Fiesta through the French lanes, keeping his distance. That man in the Skoda was a villain, he was as sure of that as he was of his own parentage. All he needed was proof - that's what his commanding officer had said. Get some evidence of some committed crimes and things would look pretty good for Baxter Collins. Only a year in the force and promotion could already be prescribed; not bad for a twenty-three year old rookie.

Baxter considered his prey once more. Johnny Cartwright was a small time drug supplier, a slippery customer who had a network of dealers in the Birmingham area. The Drug Squad had pulled him in three times already this year, but never managed to hold him on a charge of anything more than possession of a tiny bit of cannabis. And then Baxter had got involved and this time he had spilled the beans. After some clever interrogation techniques, they had ascertained that the woman in the Droitwich council offices had been the key. Helen Cartwright was Johnny's elder sister and, by his own confession in the cells, she was his main supplier. The woman seemed fairly innocent and Baxter didn't believe him at first, until he had tailed her and overheard her discussing one of their pick-ups in Europe with her colleague. From then on, Baxter had a pretty good idea that her and this Trevor Hard were as guilty as OJ Simpson himself. After a couple of attempts, Baxter had managed to persuade his boss that he was hot on the trail of a major drugs ring, and that it would require him to tail a suspect over into Europe, undercover.

The only other real evidence they had to go on was a coded message that the man had inserted into a local newspaper, obviously meant for his contact to read, but well disguised. Although they hadn't managed to crack the code, Baxter had a team of experts - well a team of only one expert to be precise, as budgets were tight these days - trying to decode the sordid conversations of the men who answered it. He reached for his mobile phone to check for any progress.

'Rich? Anything more on those calls?' he questioned the officer who answered on the first ring.

'Another call today, Bax, about half an hour ago. Similar to the others. Only this one wanted to meet tomorrow in Borsall Heath at 7pm. No mention of France though. Are you sure you have the right suspect?'

Baxter ignored the question. 'Did you trace the caller?'

'Yeah, Jason..,' Baxter heard a shifting of paperwork as the officer looked up the details. 'Jason Tully, local businessman, thirty-one, white, lives in Moseley, no previous.'

'OK, bring him in,' he replied, 'and grill him like the others. You know the drill.' He pressed the red button to end the call, narrowly avoiding an oncoming car as he swerved back on to the right side of the road. 'Local businessman, eh?' he muttered to himself, 'could this be our man?' Half smiling, he picked up his phone again.

'Baxter here, Sir. On French soil and tailing the suspect.' He listened hopefully to his boss's reply before continuing. 'I managed to get some of his belongings, a belt with some cash in it. Nothing else inside it, just 300 euros. Should I send it to you for forensics, Sir?' Baxter's face reddened as the voice on the other end raised its tone. 'Stealing? But he is a criminal, Sir. What?' He pulled the car over to the side of the road. 'Well, I took it as evidence, Sir,' Baxter protested innocently.

He waited until the voice finished shouting.

'Give it back? Yes, Sir. I heard you loud and clear!'

*

Jason Tully was none too keen to accompany the officer to the station, especially this morning of all mornings. He was certainly not keen on the charge that the officer had started to read out to him in a loud condescending voice outside his front door. Reluctantly he went along in the back of the police car, looking sheepishly around as he stepped out through the garden to see a few twitching curtains in neighbouring flats. They had nothing on him, he knew that. A phone call to answer a newspaper advert wasn't illegal was it?

After half an hour, Jason whistled cockily as he pranced down the concrete steps outside the giant police station in the old Jewellery Quarter in Birmingham, glancing back at the huge ugly building soaring up towards the sky, completely out of keeping with the properties around it.

'Thanks for the lift, boys!' he called out loud. Jason checked his watch, he still had plenty of time to make his appointment this morning, and this was going to be the big one. After a brief coffee in a grubby café on the corner of Grafton Road, Jason tugged up the collar of his leather jacket and stepped towards Hockley High Street to meet his contact, whistling a happy tune to himself. Jason considered today would be the best move he had made in his career.

It just so happened to be his last.

*

Try recognised the man instantly. Sure, he had a different hat on now and sunglasses, but he was pretty certain it was him, the one he had seen in the toilet on that godforsaken ship. He wouldn't have clocked him, but for bumping into him as he stepped down the narrow passageway after using the toilet in this service station for a more comfortable purpose. Even then, he wouldn't have taken much notice until the man had sort of fondled him as they squeezed past.

Is that what gay people do?

'*Maybe that was some sort of signature thing*,' said his conscience, '*you know, like a Masonic handshake or a sheep-farmer's nod?*'

Try was no expert in such matters, nor did he intend to be, but why was he being pursued by a gay man? Should he go and speak to him? Maybe clear the matter up? Instinctively, Try cleared his throat and counted to three before he spoke to the cashier as she handed him his change.

'Merci,' he said in a very deep voice, attempting to sound like Barry White.

Except this made him cough, blurting out his sick-stained breath all over the poor girl as she stepped back in embarrassment. 'Oh sorry,' he said, in English, sounding more like Snow White this time.

Hurriedly grabbing his tube of mints and bottle of water, Try headed through the heavy glass doors and out into the balmy warmth of the car-park, glancing back to see if the man was following. Behind him, his pursuer casually ambled to the counter with a pack of sandwiches as he desperately fumbled for the car keys in his pocket. Then Try walked towards his car in the sort of walk that is pretending not to be a run, almost skipping his feet across the tarmac like one of those Olympic athletes - had he been in an Olympic walking race, he definitely would have been disqualified – until he reached the Skoda and ripped open the driver's door. Terrified and somewhat paranoid, he dived in and groped for the ignition, eventually managing to get the engine started. But, due to his still getting used to the clutch control on his new car, the Skoda's engine screamed up to 5000 revs as he made sure he didn't stall it this time, before his foot jumped off the clutch pedal just a bit too hastily and the wheels screeched into a spin on the dry tarmac like the start of a rally.

In a parking space not far away, a gendarme in an immaculate dark blue uniform astride an immensely powerful motor-cycle dropped the visor on his helmet. Underneath him, the machine's engine sparked into life and he was just about to follow the rapidly departing Skoda when another man ran out from the shop, jumped into a Ford and gave chase. Raising one bushy eyebrow inside his gleaming helmet, Officer Broule switched on his radio, and considered summoning back-up.

Baxter Collins had visions of taking a powerful unmarked squad car across Europe, one of those cushy ones that the traffic department used to while away the hours on motorway bridges instead of doing proper police work. But there were the cut-backs, always the bloody cutbacks. Instead he had ended up with a crumby little Ford Fiesta that had long since been round the clock and was only really used by the Super's wife when hers was in for service. Baxter's right ankle was starting to ache as he forced the pedal down into the floor, trying to get the damn thing to go faster as he did his best to keep the Skoda in his sights. His mind raced as well. Had Hard recognised him, he wouldn't be that smart, surely? The drug-squad officer had done his best to push the money belt under Hard's jacket but he had been unsuccessful and, as the man had struggled past him, it had fallen to the floor into a puddle of oily water. Baxter glanced down at the bedraggled object on the seat beside him, convinced that it could be used as evidence. Ever since that time in the interview with Cartwright, he hadn't thought a lot of his boss. The man didn't have stamina, didn't have the tenacity to grind down a suspect and get results; didn't have the balls for it. Well, he would show them about balls. Baxter Collins had been a brilliant student at the academy, passing his course with flying colours and the highest commendation. That was how he had progressed straight to the drug-squad. No pounding the beat in a pointy hat for this officer, none of that nonsense chasing shop-lifters through the mall on pathetic mountain bikes. No sir. Narcotics! That was where it was at; that was where the keys to the future lay. Baxter knew all about Narcs. When he was not out catching criminals, American cop shows on TV were his only source of entertainment.

Meanwhile, Try was desperately doing mathematic calculations in his head as he gripped the leather steering wheel with white knuckles. It had been a long time since he had done mental arithmetic as nowadays he used calculators and spreadsheets, although generally the answer involved the number three.

Three divided by five times eight.

That was the problem he was working on to occupy his mind.

Or was it five divided by eight times three?

There was definitely a ratio between three, five and eight that calculated the difference between miles and kilometres, he knew that much, as he watched the needle rising on the speedometer on the dashboard in front of him to 90 miles per hour. Three times nine was twenty seven, divided by five times eight was... He counted the figures out on his fingers. That seemed about right, if you moved the decimal point. Did that mean he was breaking the speed limit? Try wasn't completely sure.

It had been a while since he had got back onto the auto-route, after pulling three hundred more euros out of a cash machine in a small town he had already forgotten the name of. First, he had phoned Helen to tell her about the stolen money belt and she had reassured him that he would be able to claim it back on his holiday insurance. Try had dug out the insurance document from a plastic wallet in his suitcase, scanning the small-print three times before eventually being satisfied that he could go ahead and draw out some more money. Then he had checked the map and rejoined the motorway near Rouen, at junction 3, collecting a small ticket from the third booth. All would have been going to plan, had he not bumped into the man in the service station.

Trying to put it from his mind, he turned on the radio again, checking the rear view mirror as the Skoda sped along at close to top speed. Some distance behind he thought he saw a motorbike that he had noticed earlier. His mind returned to the math calculation and he was just getting to a different answer when his mobile phone rang again.

'Where the fuck is it?' snarled a voice on the other end.

2

Like many war babies, Brian Hard's early years had been tough. Growing up in suburban Birmingham, England, his father had been a miner until the outbreak of the Second World War had enticed him off in a Lancaster bomber to Northern Europe, never to return. With little or no qualifications, young Brian had enlisted in the RAF on leaving school and been posted to some remote camp in East England. There he had spent many years attempting to become a pilot before the despondency of continually failing the flying exams resigned him to the fact that 'firmly on the ground' was where he belonged. As an engineer he had been posted to Northern Africa and it was there that he had met a pretty young Albanian girl called Anya who, much to his mother's aversion, very soon became his wife.

The two of them then moved into a regulation house on an RAF base in Mid Wales and it was in this lonely town that their only child Trevor had been born. Anya had been a simple soul with simple principles, insisting that they carry on the Albanian traditional of naming their son after his grandfather, Richard Yashati. It had never occurred to her that this tradition may have not been in her son's best interest until, at the age of 7, his school master paid them a visit to say that the boy was constantly getting into fights in the school playground and was the brunt of rather too many jokes amongst the local taffs. Around that time, the RAF in their infinite wisdom had decided to promote Brian to the rank of officer. At first the couple were elated by the news until it transpired that it would mean them relocating to an airbase in Germany, just for a few years, and then possibly to Scotland or the Middle East after that. One of the few perks of this promotion was that sons of RAF officers would get a good education, paid for by the Ministry of Defence, and so it was that Trevor Richard Yashati Hard was enrolled in Brocton Boarding School for boys, aged 8.

Brocton was a modest school compared to its larger public-school counterparts such as Eton and Harrow. Those prestigious establishments focussed on turning out politicians, great sportsmen and leaders of men. With some fairly second rate staff and third rate facilities, Brocton was more concerned with turning out boys with good enough qualifications to drive a tractor, enter the building trade or - something which was largely encouraged - join the forces. After a couple of predominantly unhappy years in its junior department, TRY, as he was now known, progressed to a boarding house in the main school at the age of 10, where the matronly figure of Mrs Abbots was replaced by a housemaster from a more bygone era. Despite the western world now catapulting towards a 1980's degree of civilisation, Pollock House was still rooted firmly in the 1940's and run with military efficiency and cleanliness by Major Peter Edwards. It was common knowledge amongst the boys that the ferocious Major Edwards had seen war service in the front line, although nobody was ever actually quite clear where that front line was, nor exactly what had happened during his time there. All they knew was that it didn't pay to cross him or even look him too sharply in the eye, or else it was 'see me in my study at 8pm'.

Try had visited that study far more times than is good for any normal boy, standing terrified in the queue in his towelling dressing-gown, awaiting his turn to be beaten with a chalked bamboo cane, while hearing the echoes of whacks and screams pinging around the dining room. It wasn't just the housemaster that beat him either, as the pecking order of an antiquated and traditional school such as Brocton afforded the older boys to gain their confidence to graduate into the real world by flexing their muscles on the younger ones. On the rugby fields of Wales he took his punishment too, being adorned with the shirt of full-back, a garment and responsibility that was at least three sizes too big for a seven stone weakling such as himself. Brocton School, and its housemaster in particular, favoured larger stronger boys in just about every facet of its inadequate education system and it would be fair to say that it didn't really favour Trevor, ne Try, Hard.

At the age of 16, armed with 3 o'levels in history, chemistry and the ever-useful woodwork, Try gleefully left Brocton, never to return. By this time, his parents had moved into a new sprawling 'experimental' city called Telford in Shropshire. The idea for the city of Telford was concocted in the drug-crazed mind of an over zealous labour minister during the mid-seventies. Sold to the country as an 'over-spill' town for Birmingham's ever increasing population, it offered new architecture and a new future for those who were prepared to move with the times. The fact that this new architecture was constructed solely from precast grey concrete and that the new future offered absolutely zero employment was conveniently missed out from the marketing brochure as hoards of prospectors ambled blindly into its modern grey surroundings.

For a sixteen year old boy with a strange name, a posh accent and still wearing seventies fashion, the new future offered little more than the one Try had just escaped from. Not for the first time in his life, local boys found him a fairly easy target for their aggression, and this time there was no headmaster on hand to confiscate their flick-knives. Terrified to attend any dances or nightclubs in the town, the only interaction that Try had with girls of his own age were the student nurses in the new futuristic but grossly underfunded hospital, as they sympathetically tended to his bruises and cuts.

After a final one hour visit to the careers office at school, run by one Major Edwards, Try had no idea of what he wanted to do in the way of work, as long as it didn't involve the only career that his house-master and career mentor had suggested; the Army. However, goaded by his father and encouraged by brightly coloured pictures of smiling rugged men with fashionable looking moustaches in the brochure that Major Edwards had sent him home with, Try reluctantly made an appointment at the Army office. Before he could re-gather what little decorum and self-respect that his misplaced upbringing had left him with, he had signed the forms and enlisted for three years as a soldier.

Within a week, Try had once again relocated, this time from his tiny bedroom within a square box that masqueraded as modern housing in Shropshire for yet another dormitory, now on an Army barracks in deepest Yorkshire. Desperate to keep his embarrassing title a secret, Try introduced himself to the other young men as Trev, Kev and even Ritchie in an attempt to make friends with his fellow recruits. His disguise lasted all of 3 hours until, on the first visit to their billet from Sergeant Harris, his cover was blown amidst sniggering laughter as the words: TRY HARD were not only yelled at 40 decibels directly into his left ear, but taken on as a new motto for the whole platoon.

In the USA, before, during and after the Second World War, posters of Uncle Sam wanting YOU were commonplace as the State department constantly recruited young men to give their lives towards the protection of their beloved country. Similar campaigns were much more subtle in Britain, with sedate slogans such as Dig for Victory and Hush, Walls have Ears now well past their sell-by appeal. During years of depression and economic suffering, joining the forces was an attractive option for young men with little prospects, but in the opportunistic eighties, not only was the world not at war, but government cutbacks no longer offered the levels of pay that matched that of any but the lowest paid jobs in the commercial sector. Basically, the Armed Forces were going through change. This is possibly one of the reasons that Try had managed to pass the entrance exam and very likely the same reason that the Royal Light Infantry, 16 Platoon, was made up largely of losers and down-and-outs.

'Cam on, you 'orrible drop-outs, TRY HARD!' boomed the sergeant at the shaven-headed squadies, while attempting to get them to march in time. Fortunately, after 3 years being in the cadet force at school, marching was something that Try had already mastered. 'Try Hard to be like Try Hard!' yelled Sergeant Harris at his confused recruits. Very soon, the words Try Hard had been adopted throughout the whole company, and had even been sanctioned by the Colonel himself. For a while, this gave Try a sort of minor celebrity status, and his own picture even appeared in the revamped recruitment brochure.

There is a theory that being a B-List celebrity is not an attractive position to many folks, in the same way that being a school milk-monitor or traffic-warden only appeals to a very select few of the human race. The reason is thus: Wannabe minor celebrities are despised by anyone with real ambition or bona-fide celebrity status and considered as limpets, trying to cling on to the arse of success in an attempt to drag themselves along with it without actually giving any value. Of equal importance, the minor celeb is ridiculed by those without enough talent to make it above their own amoebeotic miserable level of existence. Fundamentally, unless one can use one's famed status to rise above the disposition, jealousy and vindication of ones peers, being a minor celebrity is asking for a kicking, especially if one is in the Army. Hence, life for a young man called Try Hard was not much fun in Platoon 16.

During his later years at Brocton School, the weekly all-too-sparse timetable had been padded out by a double lesson of sociology taught by a virtually insane ex-priest with an over-active imagination. Answering purely to the name of Bunce - no first name and no title - this relic of the sixties hippy era instilled in the boys his bizarre theories about how the mind, the world and not least, the human race really worked. Many of his ideas were induced by hallucinogenic substances and most were too outlandish for the boys to even comprehend, as they whiled away the school hours staring into space as old Bunce droned on and on about God being an alien and all Politicians being disciples of the Devil himself. However, in the interest of not going completely insane himself, Try had taken a more than active attention to one of Bunce's more reasonable propositions, something Bunce called the Rule of Three. Basically, this unbalanced theory portrayed that everything that happened in the world, and in the worlds beyond it, could be divided by, or at the very least, blamed on, the number three. Bunce had explained it in such intimate - although highly un-proven - detail that Try had adopted the whole philosophy into his young, confused and rather unstable mind, where it would live and fester. From that moment on, he not only believed that death and buses always arrived in threes, but world disasters, sausages, parking spaces, street-lamps and girls as well. In fact, in just about everything he experienced, Try's subconscious mind would catalogue it into a series, awaiting the third recurring instance so that he could tick the box to satisfy himself that the sequence of three had ended. He even considered the fact that he had three forenames to be because of the same said ruling. If nothing else, this volatile belief brightened up what was otherwise a rather dull life for Trevor R Y Hard.

The ROT, as Try referred to it, was the reason that he had signed to the Army for three years. It could also be attributed to the fact that within three minutes of being in the service, someone had punched him, as well as the three hours it took for them to find out his real name. Now, with the wrath of some of his brutal colleagues in the platoon bearing down on him, coupled with the distain of the majority of his superiors, Try believed that three weeks was all the time he could survive in Her Majesty's forces before he would be killed by his own side without even seeing action. With this in mind, on his twenty-first day at Willingsdale army barracks, a rather battered Try had applied first to Sergeant Harris, then to his Lieutenant and finally to the Colonel himself, to be discharged. The fact that each application had been turned down had come as no surprise to Try, who then considered that under his own ruling, he was confined to death within the ranks unless he could make it to the next ROT milestone, that of three months.

For once, fortune fell on the side of the less fortunate, as Try fell from the climbing wall, dislocating his left shoulder and being carted off on a stretcher by two burly soldiers to the sanatorium, screaming in pain. For many, a fall from a ten foot wall and an agonising bone injury would not count as fortune of any kind, especially while a wrench-handed army medical officer investigated his shoulder with all the sensitivity of a ball-pin hammer. It wasn't until the man was relieved from his shift and replaced with a rather fresh-faced female medical recruit that not only was Try's broken shoulder diagnosed but, when she eventually embarrassingly removed all his clothes, many of his other injuries as well. Within three hours, Try was driven the thirty miles to Harrogate general hospital and placed in ward three. After three days recovering, a discharge note from the Army arrived at his bedside. Exactly three months after he had joined up Try was, once again, a civilian.

Despite his own failings years earlier, Mr Hard was none too sympathetic to a son who hadn't even been able to pass first muster in the Army corp, although Try's mother did wince when she saw some of the bruising. It became fairly evident that he was not welcome to move back into the family home in Telford and that he should perhaps seek alternative accommodation. For a young man with no friends, male or female, who had prematurely left boarding school and then dropped out of the army, there was really only one place left for him to go. Try got a government job. For this one, irrespective of his lack of qualifications, he was possibly over-qualified when, within two weeks, he was enrolled and inaugurated as an office junior at Droitwich town council, a position he could hold if he so chose, for life.

Try had been there, for better or worse, ever since.

During the last 22 years, Droitwich town council offices had undergone extensive change, being moved from a Victorian brick building full of stale air and rats, to a more modern affair with large windows and a janitor. Unfortunately, during that very same period, the work ethic of its staff had not moved forward one iota. In fact, in certain areas, they had gone backwards. Sure, Try's initial boss had retired due to a stress-related disease some years back and one of his colleagues in accounts had reputedly died of boredom, but generally, the same staff endured the very same mundane existence that they had done when he joined. Since the introduction of computers, the number of staff it took to run a small unimportant Midlands town had declined from 22 to 12, as jobs were lost and no new ones created. This meant that, by and large, after 22 years in the position, Try was still one of the youngest in the office. The fact that, regardless of their real age, all its employees acted, spoke and dressed like they were 55, Try included, could not deter them from still treating him as the office boy. Basically, for the last 22 years, Try had spent the majority of his working career counting paperclips and playing solitaire.

3

Try pressed a button to put the caller on speakerphone as he attempted to turn down the radio.

'Where is what?'

'Don't give me that bollocks. You know what. Now where the fuck is it?'

Before he left the office, in the interest of not being forgotten while he was away on holiday, Try had left his mobile phone number written on a post-it note stuck to his computer screen, in case of emergencies. Was this someone from work calling him now? Maybe they were looking for the photocopier paper? Since he had made the rash decision to tidy up the stationary cupboard after the Christmas break, the location of the photocopier paper had frequently haunted his daily job. It didn't sound like anyone he knew in the office, and he knew pretty well all of them. And another thing, members of Droitwich town council offices didn't swear, well not like that anyway. OK, Jeffrey had cursed a little bit, when he had broken his fingernail in the ring-binder at Easter, but he hadn't used the F word. And this caller had definitely used that. Twice.

'I am sorry, I am not gay. It was a mistake!'

The line went quiet for a second, before the snarling voice came back, louder and snarlier this time.

'What the fuck are you on about? I couldn't care if you were a cross-dressing fucking pervert. I just want my goods. And I want them fucking now. Get it. Fuckwit?'

Try could never recall being called a fuckwit before, as his mind somersaulted through permutations of who this caller might be. Eventually, it settled for what could be the only obvious solution. Gathering his vocal chords back into their correct order, Try told the man of his conclusion.

'I am sorry, but you must have the wrong number. Goodbye!' In his attempt to press the red button to end the call, his mobile phone fell from his hand and wedged under the driving seat and Try could still hear the caller shouting out his obscenities on the other end as he swerved the Skoda across two lanes in his attempts to pick it up again. At that moment, a blue light started flashing behind him and, glancing up through his side mirror, Try saw a large police motorbike looming by his side. For the second time in 3 hours, an officer pointed a leather gloved finger, firstly at him and then at the side of the road.

'Oh fuck!' were the only words he could utter as mild panic set it.

'I'll give you Oh Fuck, you fucking Fuck!' came a reply from under his seat.

Just as the officer pulled open the Skoda door, Try managed to locate his mobile phone and end the abusive call. Officer Broule raised his menacing dark visor and glowered down at the phone in Try's shaking hand and then shook his head. Try let out a nervous smile when he realised the offence he must have committed.

'Oh this?' he said, 'I was just getting it from under the seat. It fell down, you see. I wasn't using it while driving, honest! It was hands-free, officer.'

Immediately, the shrill speaker played its French ringtone again and briefly Try glanced down at it, but this time he ignored the call. Officer Broule glared at him, his head cocked on one side.

'Are you going to answer eet?' Try was quite impressed that the man had a reasonable grasp of English, although his accent needed a little polish.

'No. Wrong Number!'

'Ow do you know it ees a wrong number? You did not answer eet?' What had been a nervous smile now morphed into a terrified grimace on Try's face as the large police officer took the phone from his hand, studied it for a few seconds, before pressing the green button and holding it to his ear.

'Oui, allo?'

'Now you fucking listen to me, you fucking idiot.' Officer Broule raised an eyebrow as he continued to listen to the seamlessly linked English swearwords snarling at him. Eventually, when he got a chance to but in to the conversation, he uttered a short sentence in perfect English which stopped the caller in his tracks.

'This is the police. Oo is this?' Instantly, the line went dead, as the unimpressed officer handed Try back his telephone.

'Wrong number!' he said again, trying his smile once more.

'One 'undred and forty-two kilometres per hour!'

'Was I? Oh Gosh. I didn't think that this car....'

'One 'undred and forty-two kilometres per hour, driving when using the telephone, driving dangerously....' He stopped, as if gathering his French thoughts into English before pointing to the phone. 'And now..zis!' Try gulped a lump into his throat and said nothing.

'Well, what do you 'ave to say?'

'Sorry?' said the council worker, pathetically. 'It wont 'appen again?' Officer Broule's eyes narrowed.

'What will not 'appen again?'

'All of it. Er, none of it. Look!' He threw the phone down on to the floor of the passenger side of the car, as if to prove a point. The officer looked around, clocking the cars passing by, as all the drivers slowed to check out what was going on with his latest arrest.

'Why so fast? Hmmm?'

'I didn't know I was going that fast,' blurted out Try, still clutching at a hope of getting away with his little problem. 'It's the thirds, you see. I couldn't work out the third!' In front of him, the officer pulled out a notebook, licking a small pencil and starting to write while Try considered his ROT theory. That was twice in three hours he had been questioned by the police. That made it 100% likely it would happen again. He would make sure of it.

'Turds..' said the Officer out loud, writing it down.

'Thirds!' corrected the Try, 'Th-th-th!' Instinctively, the confused gendarme stepped back to avoid the stench of Try's rancid breath.

'Qu'est que c'est, thirds?'

'Bunce's theory of ROT!'

'ROT!' said the policeman, writing it down. He was just about to add calmly that, after committing four offenses, this driver had better stop insulting him when a walkie-talkie radio crackled into life on his motor-cycle parked in front of the Skoda. Raising his eyebrows to the heavens, the officer strode away from the car and answered the call, nodded his head a bit more urgently a couple of times, then returned again.

'Mister English. You must drive more carefully, and be even more careful with your language!' Try nodded eagerly. 'Now go on your way before I put you in jail!'

*

'Now we're getting somewhere!' replied Baxter excitedly, smoothing his black hair as he spoke to his colleague on the phone. 'I knew it. I just knew it was him! Call it intuition. Nah, hell, just call it skill!' While he was praising himself, the man on the other end of the line interrupted Baxter with a question. 'Where is he now?' he repeated. 'Well, he has just been pulled over for speeding by an interfering traffic cop but I don't think they will hold him because he wasn't going fast enough. He'll just be cautioned. Gotta go, Rich, here he comes now. Keep me posted will ya. Ciao.' Baxter crunched the Ford into first gear and pulled out from the layby, once again in pursuit of a yellow Skoda on English number plates as it cruised by in the slow lane.

'So, at last a call had come from one of their known suspects?' Baxter's brain reacted smugly to this, as though the arrest would now just be a forgone conclusion. This time he followed the car from a safe distance, intrigued as to where his suspect was heading to and who he was going to meet. An arrest could wait a little longer.

In his head, the young detective ran through what he could remember about a profile of the caller. His real name was Maydon Hornsey but everyone knew him as Max, even the force. Max had been busted umpteen times and had a track record in armed crimes listing on to two sheets of paper. For a while, Winson Green Prison had been this villain's second home, where he could enlist most of the inmates to get him just about anything he needed. Some of the warders were on his payroll too. In short, Max was a well known thug amongst Birmingham's underworld; a gangster of the first order. Amongst the local police force, there was suspicion that Max Hornsey's enterprise ran to national and even international proportions, although there was little proof. About a year ago, he had been photographed talking to a man who had connections in the human trafficking trade, but Baxter knew little more about it. Illegal immigrants were plentiful in the Midlands area, that was for sure, but all that stuff was handled by a different division and the information kept very tight. He checked the notes on his pad again. 'Where the fuck is it? Where are my fucking goods?' For GOODS read DRUGS. Max had phoned Hard about a shipment of drugs and he was quite angry about it. More fool Hard, if he had double-crossed Max Hornsey. That was a good way to get yourself killed. And one thing that Baxter really didn't want was his suspect dead; not until he had bagged him for narcotics crimes anyway. As he saw it, Hard was obviously heading over Europe to make a pick-up. All he had to do was to tail him, witness the deal, allow him to get back to England and pick the right moment. Then the Drug Squad could bust him, Max and hopefully Jimmy Cartwright all at the same time, with possibly a good few other villains in the process. Baxter Collins tingled with excitement at the thought of it. Lost in his thoughts, he nearly missed the fact that his suspect was indicating to pull into yet another service station.

Why did this man keep stopping?

Had he got a bladder problem or something?

Maybe it was the drugs? Perhaps Hard was stopping to take some more drugs, the dirty swine. Baxter was tempted to arrest him right now, and give him the kicking he deserved. Instead, he followed the Skoda cautiously and watched it park up near the main door. To stay out of sight, he drove the Ford around the back, and nestled it between two large lorries, one of which still had its engine running. Here he could sit and wait for the man to come back out again, without being seen. Better still, he would get out of his car and go and check the Skoda over while Hard was inside. Maybe the door might be unlocked, and he could push the man's money belt inside?

Inside the service station Try did indeed have a bladder problem, one that had been induced by fear and blind panic. Being stopped and interviewed by the French police was only a small part of the problem. It had been the phone call that scared him at first and, despite him desperately persuading himself that it had been a wrong number, the voice on the other end had flooded Try with dread. But that wasn't the only problem, because now he was convinced he was being followed. At first he thought he was imagining it, when he occasionally saw a familiar blue car in the rear-view mirror, but after he had passed it parked on the shoulder of the motorway and seen it pull out behind him, he was 100% certain. The man who had phoned him and sworn continuously at him was now following him through France, wanting his stuff back. Or if it wasn't him personally, he had one of his men doing it for him.

'*You're being paranoid!*' said his logical conscience.

'*Just because you're paranoid doesn't mean that they're not out to get you?*' said the sceptical part of the same conscience, with practiced reverberation - whatever that is.

Since the call, Try had instantly switched off his mobile phone, hoping the caller would give up on him and forget the whole thing. Then he had spent the next hour driving at 85 kph raking through his memory to identify whose stuff he might inadvertently have. It must have been something to do with that man he had seen in the last petrol station, the one who had fondled him as they bumped together in the corridor. Perhaps the man wasn't gay at all. Maybe he had planted something on him, some booty. Try checked all his pockets but all he could come up with was a packet of chewing gum which he couldn't remember buying, but he didn't think it would be that. No, it had to be something else, something smaller perhaps, maybe a microchip? Nervously, he stood in the small cubicle, thinking though his next move. Hurriedly, he took off his jacket, rolled it up neatly and, balancing by one foot on the bowl of the toilet, pushed it behind a large metal pipe near the ceiling. If whatever the man was looking for had been planted on his jacket, then at least he could tell the caller where it was, without having to meet the fearsome brute. That made him feel a little better. Next, peering anxiously through a crack in the door to check no one was waiting outside, he opened the toilet door and started to make his way back to his car, trying not to look suspicious. Within seconds, the fear returned as he glanced out of the window across the forecourt to see the same man loitering near his car, possibly testing the door handle. Slinking back behind a gurgling coffee machine, he waited until his pursuer had casually sauntered off back towards the lorry park with his hands in his pockets. Had he planted something else? A tracker device, perhaps? Or a bomb even. It didn't bear thinking about.

With his terror now merging into unmitigated paranoia, Try counted to three, before strolling towards the Skoda with the gait of one who is being inconspicuous, dropped to his knees and checked underneath it. Thankfully there was no parcel or anything suspicious. Then, after checking each of the doors in turn, including the boot, he looked around to see if he was being watched, before displaying a shrug with both his palms outstretched. If a man was looking to retrieve something from him, then he wanted it to be known that he hadn't found it.

Baxter watched this with interest, from behind a nearby bush. Hard was certainly acting suspiciously. Had this been the pick up point? Suddenly the detective was annoyed with himself that maybe he had warned off the contact. Perhaps someone had seen him near the Skoda and decided not to make the exchange. Was that what this was about? Hard was making a show of it, knowing he was being watched? Maybe this was some sort of signal.

Over many years, the English and the French have had a running battle with each other over all sorts of things; be it over wealth and power, beef and lamb or in more recent times, the lorries and trains. Rules had been imposed on French lorry drivers about the hours they drove, especially on British soil, which had angered quite a few of them. Seeing a small British car parked in what was essentially a French lorry bay was too much of a temptation from even the mildest-mannered trucker and when Baxter returned to it, the Ford was hemmed in on all sides and would be for some time. From this moment on, Baxter's chase of his suspect was over. Behind the Ford, a giant lorry filled the remainder of the parking bay, with no sign of its driver anywhere. In front of him it was the same. Looking under the gantry of a trailer on his left side, Baxter saw the yellow Skoda drive back on to the motorway and let out an angry curse. Not yet totally defeated, in a desperate attempt to move one of the vehicles around him, he climbed up to the cab of the one which still had its engine running and banged on the window. Dim light glowed inside of the cab which was covered by an orange curtain, hiding the interior from view.

'Open up. I need you to move this wagon. Now!' This time he banged his fist loudly on the door. On receiving no response, Baxter tried the door handle, finding out, to his own surprise that is wasn't locked. 'Hello? Anyone in there?' The door opened towards him and he climbed the ladder, poking his head under the curtain. 'Come on, you need to move...' All of a sudden, Baxter's world went black, as the thick end of a metal wheel-brace caught him just above the ear.

La Rochelle 367 kms said the overhead sign. Try adjusted his foot on the accelerator pedal, slowing down slightly as he ran the mathematical calculation through his overactive and confused brain. That would mean he could make it in precisely three hours, if he drove at exactly

122.3 kph. For the last hour, he had been constantly checking his rear-view mirror for the blue car, but there had been no sign of it. The stress of looking up to the mirror and back to the road had put an ache in his neck so he had now limited himself to only looking every three minutes. Should he phone ahead and let his landlady know he would be there by 6pm, in time for supper? His last email to Madame Meatier had told her that it would be 7 o'clock, so he might be unexpected. But then, to phone her would mean switching his phone back on, and Try wasn't sure he wanted to do that in case the nasty caller phoned him again or, even worse, had left him a message.

Maybe it had all been a mistake? It was possible. In his past, Try had often been on the wrong end of sheer coincidence, like the time when he was supposed to meet that fat girl on a date and she had been late. The chances of two girls called Julia waiting for a chap outside Bloxwich cinema were pretty rare, but for them both to be wearing a red scarf too, that was highly improbable. When he had gotten back to work after a trip hospital with a suspected broken jaw, Try had set up a spreadsheet to calculate the actual probability of it happening and it ran into hundreds of thousands to one. So a man bumping into him in a corridor on a motorway service station, and then following him by car to the next one was almost acceptable odds, probably below 100-1. The fact that the same man had been sniffing around his car could be explained away as well. Let's face it, it was a nice car, the second from top of the range. And a great colour too. Maybe the chap was just drawn to the colour, and couldn't resist testing the door handles to see how smooth the mechanism was. Try checked the clock on the dashboard; only two and a half minutes had passed so he forced himself not to check the mirror. At least that man had stopped following him now, as far as he could tell. Behind him, all the other traffic had looked normal, all on French number-plates minding their own business. Another probability that Try was working on, was that of a caller dialling the wrong number, twice. Generally phone numbers were 10 digits long, so to accidentally dial one digit wrong was a simple one in ten chance. Anyone could make that error. In fact, realistically, the first number would be zero, and it was unlikely that any caller would get that one wrong, so it was only a one in nine probability. But to do it again, that was a bit further out in the odds tables. (1 in 9) multiplied by (1 to the power of nine), he reckoned, and that could run into thousands of percent. Persuaded by his own sense of inquisitiveness, Try reached down and picked up the phone from the seat, glancing into its empty screen for a second. Then he remembered the time, damn, 3 minutes and eleven seconds had passed. Drawing in a deep breath, he checked the mirror again. Still no blue Ford. He let his breath out again.

There were just the same old cars that had been there most of the way; a grey Mercedes; some kind of four-wheel-drive in magenta, and a motor bike. No, that didn't look like any danger. Holding his breath again, Try held a thumb on the red button of the mobile phone until the screen lit up, before setting it into the hands-free cradle on the dashboard. After a full minute, no messages appeared and he relaxed a bit more. See, it was all just a simple mix up.

Making sure he kept a constant speed, Try scrolled through the numbers on the telephone until he came to Madame Meatier, cleared his throat and then hit the dial button. After three rings, it picked up.

'Oui? Allo?' said a husky French voice.

'Ah. Hello Mrs Meatier, this is Trevor Hard, travelling down from England.' Try made it sound like he was travelling down from space with his opening introduction.

'Met-i-air. C'est Madame Met-i-air, Monsieur.'

'Er, yes, of course. Mrs Met-i-air. Right. Um, have you got dinner?'

'Pardon Monsieur, I cannot 'ear you.'

Try raised his voice. 'Er, I will be arriving in time for dey-gon-ay! Will that be alright?'

'Dey-gon-ey?'

'Er, yes. Dinner...?'

The voice on the other end softened into a shrill laughter. 'Dejeuner? Non, dejeuner ees finish.'

'Er, this evening. I will be there by six pm.'

'What ees six-pee-em?'

Try was getting confused already. 'Er six ocklock, dix-huit heure, can I have some dinner?'

'Dix-huit heures? Ah oui, d'accord, some dinner, oui c'est ca, diner. Mais oui, Monsieur.'

Try considered this as a yes, although he had struggled with most of the words. 'Merci, Madamme Meatier, I mean Met-i-air.'

'A tout à l'heure!

Before he had chance to press the button to end the call, a small icon on the screen signalled that another call was coming in and Try's heart nearly stopped until he saw the name flashing up on the screen. It was Helen Cartwright.

'Hi Helen!' he shouted, once he accepted the call.

'Where are you, Trev?'

'About 3 hours away! I am doing OK.' He decided not to tell her about the incident with the man in the petrol station.

'Are you alright?'

'Yes, fine. Why shouldn't I be? I am on holiday.' A smile spread on his face when he considered this. Holiday. Yup, he had been looking forward to this for a long time.

'Trev?'

'Yes, Helen?'

'The police are looking for you!'

4

Some police were indeed looking for Trevor Hard, but they didn't include Baxter Collins, who was slumped over the steering wheel of his blue Ford Fiesta, snoring, when a ringing telephone woke him up.

'Urrrgghh?' he said into the mouthpiece, glancing around. Beside him, the big lorry had moved to be replaced by a horse-box with small windows in the side. From the inside, an eye looked out nonchalantly, chewing its cud.

'Bax? You OK?'

'Urrrgghh!' he said again, struggling to get his dry mouth to form any coherent words.

'What happened, pal, you sound rough? I've been phoning you for nearly an hour!' This last sentence snapped Baxter awake as he ran his hand over a tender bruise on the side of his head and then drew it to his mouth. Most of the blood had dried up by now, but a lot of it had matted in his hair.

'What time is it, Rich?'

'It's nearly 3 here. No idea what time it is there. Four maybe?' Baxter hooked the phone under his ear as he opened the car door and climbed out into the fresh air, glaring back at the horse in the window.

'Bastard!'

'Steady on pal, I am just the messenger!' answered his colleague on the other end of the line.

'Not you.' Baxter couldn't be bothered to tell Rich what had happened. He wasn't really sure himself as he tried to recall his last movements. 'Say that again!' he suddenly snapped, half hearing what Rich was saying.

'A murder, Bax. There has been a murder.'

'Where?' The detective's mind instantly gained focus.

'In Hockley. But that's not all. When they found the body, the last number he dialled was your old mate.'

'My old mate?'

'Hard. Your suspect, Bax. A guy gets bumped off, and the last call from his phone was to Trevor Richard Hard. Swear to God!'

'Jeez!' whistled the detective. 'What did he say?'

'Who?'

'Hard!'

'It was a few hours ago now, Bax. I already told you about the call. The stiff's name was Jason Tully.' There was silence on the line for a few seconds. 'Baxter, are you still there?' Baxter had sat down on the driver's seat with his feet on the warm tarmac. His head ached. In fact his whole body ached.

'Yeah. I'm still here.' He rubbed his chin and sighed. 'But Hard isn't!'

Standing over the sink outside the one communal toilet cubicle in the petrol station, Baxter dabbed at the blood on his head with a white handkerchief. The bleeding had started again and he was trying to stop it when a smart middle-aged lady walked in, her shiny black stilettos tapping noisily on the greasy tiled floor. When she looked at Baxter and the dripping blood, the woman let out a shriek and dashed back out from the room.

'It's OK. I'm OK!' he muttered, to nobody in particular. Within seconds, a worried looking man appeared and started gabbling to him in rapid French.

'English!' said Baxter, turning towards him, 'I am English!' The troubled man raised his eyebrows, as if to say: Damn foolish English, and then pointed to a sign on the wall depicting a man falling over surrounded by a heavy red circle. Underneath the sign was the word: Attention!

'Atten-sion!' said the man smugly, as if that explained everything. Baxter noticed he was wearing the uniform of a worker, and a small badge with his name, Jean-Luc, stencilled on it. He took a guess that this man was a cleaner of some sort. Jean-Luc followed his gaze and then spurted out another twenty words that Baxter didn't understand. Losing his cool, he grabbed the man by the lapels.

'Listen, Jean-Luc. I am OK. OK?' he pushed his face near to his. 'Now get lost!' Behind him, a woman screamed. 'And you can shut the fuck up too!' At this, she launched into a flurry of abuse, pointing at the blood on his head and waving her arms hysterically.

Before matters of a violent nature could extend themselves further, Baxter saw another man in a uniform sauntering towards him down the corridor. It was the uniform of a gendarme. 'That's all I need,' he thought to himself.

Officer Broule was 4 or 5 inches taller than Baxter Collins as he smiled down at him through a greying moustache.

'Ca va?' Baxer nodded. 'Ca va?' said the gendarme again, this time to Jean-Luc. The cleaner nodded his head, brushing down his lapels. 'Madame?'

'C'est beaucoup de sang!' she blurted out. Broule raised his eyebrows and then his eyes narrowed as he glared at her.

'Oui, ca va,' she replied finally, backing down from the situation.

'Bon!' Broule pushed past the three of them and made his way to the urinal, noisily unzipping the flies on his leather trousers.

*

'At the end of the road, turn left!' purred a woman's voice from the device on the vehicle's dashboard. Try had selected the woman personally from the built-in list of voices available in his new SatNav, because she sounded attractive, but without being threatening. Just about all his life, Try had felt threatened by attractive women. Hell, he even felt threatened by non attractive ones, sometimes more so, especially if they were in the shape of his old school matron.

Meanwhile, the last woman he had spoken to had nearly scared him to death. But it hadn't been totally unexpected. By his ROT theory, a third altercation with the police was inevitable. The police were looking for him in the office, which had something to do with a phone call. They had told her it was nothing to be alarmed about, it was just a routine. When Helen had told them he was on holiday, they had said they would be in touch and left it at that. Don't panic. Their words! And hers.

Three minutes. The device said he was just 3 minutes from his destination, and yet another woman. He hoped Madame Meatier wasn't attractive, but he rather suspected that she might be. Perspective is a strange thing which, in some way, makes everything acceptable to someone. For example, modern art can be enjoyed by people with imagination and perhaps a sense of humour, whereas others just view it as a disaster in bright colours.

Madame Meatier – pronounced met-i-air – could also be described by some, although not all, as a disaster in bright colours. By basic standards, she encompassed quite a substantial girth, although most of it was kept confined under material of considerable elasticity.

'Monsieur! Bienvenue!' Before Try had chance to reply he found himself enveloped under a mass of swirling clothes and blubber, as bright-red lips sucked a kiss on to either side of his face.

'Er, Hello, Mrs Meatier. I am Hard.' The woman's eyes nearly burst from their sockets as he spoke this unusual line of introduction.

'Mais, oui. But of course!' The voluptuous Madame threw back her head, shaking the tussles of her hair out across her shoulders. 'Of course you are, Mon Cherie!' Try swallowed a lump in his throat.

To be fair, for a woman of her years, Sylvie Meatier had kept her looks quite well. A well lived-in face displayed a few crinkled lines around the eyes, as well as larger tramlines beside her mouth which had been etched there after years of repetitive smiling. It was fairly evident that, in her younger years, she had been an extremely attractive looking woman and Sylvie's only real problem now was that she refused to believe that was no longer so appealing, nor as slim, as she once had been. As though her mirror had some magic Dorian Gray quality, when she looked into it, Sylvie saw pretty much the same woman that she had done on her twenty-fifth birthday. Possibly what she had failed to consider, was that the mirror itself was twice the size of the one of yesteryear.

'Is my car alright?'

Sylvie glanced at the Skoda. 'Monsieur 'Ard, it is a lovely colour, Now do come inside,' replied Try's new host, as she swirled around, her bright flowing clothes taking a few seconds to catch her up.

'No, I mean, err, will it be alright here…?' By the time Try had finished the sentence, Sylvie was beckoning suggestively to him from the open doorway, like a back-street hooker calling her prey towards a red light. Try resisted the urge to look behind him, his face uncontrollably turning a light shade of magenta. 'I'll, err, just get my things.'

Inside the house was a large hallway stretching away between a series of white wooden doors under an ornate archway. Try recognised it instantly from the pictures on the website, although it seemed even more splendid in real life. Somehow it reminded him of the entrance hall to Brockton school, all those years earlier, and he half expected a headmaster to step out from behind the door at the far end and scowl at him.

Madame Meatier turned a glass door handle and pushed the door inwards, again beckoning him into her lair with the smile of a seductress. As the door reached a gap of no more than a few inches, it was suddenly ripped open further, releasing a dark-coloured creature with such ferocity that its feet were powerless to gain grip on the polished parquet floor.

Very soon Try was powerless too, as a dog the size of a minivan pounded towards him, jumping up to his chest and pinning him back against a different door.

'Say hello to Napoleon, Monsieur,' she purred, as though she was introducing a small child or perhaps a pet rabbit. Napoleon was definitely neither of these things, as he slobbered his mighty tongue across Try's still reddened face as though lapping up a bowl of delicious gravy. Using all his force, he pushed the dog away by its chest, only to feel the pressure of the door behind him release and himself tumbling backwards. In a gallant attempt to keep himself on his feet, he took half a dozen shuffling back-steps until the corner of a mattress bowled him on to his back.

'Arrette!' shouted the seductive Madame, before bursting into fits of raucous laughter. As if wrestling a vicious crocodile, Try held the dog's neck away from his face long enough to wipe it with his sleeve.

'Get off me!' he wailed, recalling school days of being beaten into submission by the school bully. When he did manage to see past the dog, he could have sworn that Madame was laughing at him, as he lay helplessly under the creature. Eventually she came to his rescue.

'Napoleon! Arrette! Asseyez!' Reluctantly, the dog did as it was told, and climbed down from the bed. 'I think he likes you, Monsieur 'Ard.' This last statement was almost said in approval, as though this had been some sort of test of his worthiness. Pathetically, Try pulled himself up into a foetal position and looked back at the smiling woman. 'This is your room, and the bathroom's thought there.' With a vague wave of the wrist, she disappeared from view, with Napoleon following behind her like a puppy, leaving the door wide open.

As soon they were out of sight, Try leapt to his feet, forcing the door closed and turning the key. For a whole 30 seconds, he stood with his back against the door, quivering, as though keeping out the forces of darkness. He glanced around, taking in the over complicated décor of pink and lime green and was just about to step away from the door when the forces of darkness spoke to him again, from behind it.

'Dinner will be ready in 5 minutes, Monsieur. In the dining room!'

'Oh, thank you, err, Merci, Mrs Meatier.' Despite having not eaten for hours, he had suddenly lost his appetite. There was no doubt about it, this woman scared him. No, scared would be too mild a word, he was terrified of her, and that dog. Try sat down on the bed and rubbed his tired eyes. Somehow, he felt that although they had only just met, Madame was teasing him; taunting him even. Women often did that.

Of all the days that Try could remember, this had to have been the longest. Being robbed, followed and then pulled up by the police was enough for any man. And to top that, the police were looking for him again.

Still, for now, he was on holiday and would have to make the best of it. He would get some dinner and have an early night. This place was only somewhere to rest his head, and over the next few days he planned on getting out and seeing the area. Being a very meticulous man, Try wearily set to work, unpacking his belongings, making sure everything was neatly hung or folded, in threes, and then stowed his suitcase on top of the wardrobe.

Five minutes later, after a quick splash in the meagrely appointed bathroom, he sheepishly turned the key, opening the door a fraction and putting his eye to the crack to check the horizon for scary creatures. The coast was clear, so he stepped out into the large hallway once more, in his new leather sneakers. From the far end of the hall, he could hear the big dog howling behind one of the doors and then a thought struck him. In his haste to lock the creature - both creatures - out of his room earlier, he realised he had not gotten around to asking which was the dining room and was now confronted with the choice of 6 doors to choose from. He prayed it wouldn't be the one with the dog behind it. Before Try had chanced attempting any of the doors, one of them burst open and Madame Meatier appeared like a salamander from rock.

'Psst! Ici, Monsieur!' It was almost a whisper, not unlike a pimp calling out from a dark doorway. Again, Try resisted the urge to look behind him. 'Quick before it gets cold!' The woman glanced down at his new shoes as they squeaked loudly on the polished parquet floor and then back up to his face, shaking her head. 'Chaussures interdit dans à l'intérieur!'

Try raised his eyebrows, pretending he didn't understand, but when the woman's eyes narrowed, just for a fraction of a second, he instantly sat down on a wooden chair and undid his laces, removing the shoes and placing them in a rack by the door. There were a few other pairs of shoes there too, including a bright red pair of stilettos, which he suspected belonged to this woman.

This woman watched him, mentally tapping her foot with impatience as he approached the dining room is his white-socked feet. Then a smile came back to Madame Meatier's face as he squeezed past her while she held open the door. Inside the ornate room was a large table with carved legs, surrounded by eight chairs. On five of the eight chairs sat five people all looking at him with expectant faces. Thankfully, Napoleon wasn't one of them.

5

La Rochelle was a pretty town, even by French standards, with quaint bastide architecture positioned around an old harbour inside the Bay of Biscay on the Atlantic Ocean. For a thousand years or more, it boasted a history of French aristocracy, right up to the time when they had been inopportunely separated from their own heads. During its early years, the town had belonged to the fabulously wealthy and somewhat power-crazed Eleanor of Aquitaine who had lorded it over the French - and later the English - as she courted and married first the King of France and then King Henry II of England in her quest to become the world's first super-power. During her reign, and for a few centuries afterwards, La Rochelle had been designated as a den of iniquity to those rather unlikable fellows, the Knights Templar, who had used it for torture and other recreational purposes. Now tourists queued up to listen to stories of barbarianism of unrivalled magnitude, before flocking to the beach and enduring a massacre of the financial kind.

Amidst the older part of town the streets were narrow and, during the holiday season, often packed with revellers standing shoulder to shoulder as they spilled out from some of its lively bars and clubs. As happened with revellers everywhere, the noise and behavioural levels start fairly modestly around early evening, before steadily building into a crescendo some time after midnight.

Robbie and Zipper were two such revellers, except their revelling had started a bit earlier than most, at approximately 7.30am that day, as they downed a couple of pints in Stanstead airport while waiting for their flight. Another couple of beers in La Rochelle arrivals lounge while they waited for their bags were followed by a lunchtime visit to O'Malley's bar, just in time to catch a soccer game on TV. The bar had been rowdy and they had only just avoided being thrown out when Robbie had defused a fight between Zipper and some burly Spaniard, after his friend had fondled the man's girlfriend's petite derriere and she had slapped him. Zipper quite often did this sort of thing; he liked to touch girls, especially the pretty ones. In fact Zipper quite fancied himself with the ladies, hence the self-appointed nickname. After a gallon or more of strong lager, washed down with cheap red wine and tequila, Robbie and his pal had left the bar just about upright, and were now in search of food.

When they reached the corner of Rue du Temps, the two lads drunkenly swayed towards a couple of young girls, dressed in miniscule skirts and low cut t-shirts, who were assessing the situation.

'Ladies..' slurred the inebriated Zipper, 'come along with us, we can show you a good time.' Robbie watched his pal at work, as he hung on to a lamp-post for vertical support. 'We are going dancing. You wanna come dancing?'

The two girls glanced worriedly at each other, and then one muttered something in a foreign language. As they went to cross to other side of the road, Zipper stepped towards them, preventing their path with his arms open wide.

'Come on ladies, come see my zipper!' With that, his foot slipped from the kerb and Zipper lurched uncontrollably into one of the girls, grabbing at her clothes for support as he toppled to the ground. The offended girl screamed very loudly, as did her sister, while Zipper scrambled unsteadily back to his feet.

Robbie was at a loss to understand what occurred next, it all happened so fast. A few hundred metres away, a car door opened, a man dressed completely in black jumped out, picked up Zipper and fired four rapid punches into him. The very first punch rendered him unconscious, while the next two skilfully broke a couple of his ribs. Unfortunately for Zipper, the last one was a little more messy and splintered the young man's nose in a gush of blood and bone, as he fell sideways into a doorway.

From his vantage point amidst a few screaming bystanders, Robbie tried to focus on the man but his movements were so fast and he had gone as quickly as he had arrived, sidling back down the street and into the unmarked car, unnoticed.

Once the darkly clad man was back in his seat, his colleague spoke to him, shaking his head.

'Why do you have to fight every single battle, Serge?' The other man said nothing, just rubbed his knuckles. 'Boss said we were to stay here and keep a low profile. Just gotta watch the house, and keep outta sight!' Still there was no reply, just a grunt from the passenger seat. 'You gotta stop doing this, Serge. Let the tourists sort out their own troubles. Jeez, man, it's like being on a stakeout with Batman!'

Within a few minutes, the siren of an ambulance could be heard, making its way through the crowd, and soon the glow of a flashing red light started to appear in his rear view mirror.

'I suppose we better move, in case someone points the finger at you, huh?'

'If you want?' shrugged the darkly-clothed assassin.

'Best get you outta here, before you make it your mission to protect every young girl in the neighbourhood.' Shaking his head again, the driver put the car in gear and moved slowly off down a side-street. 'If you ask me, kids dress like that, they deserve all they get.' The way Serge said nothing, indicated that he didn't agree with his colleague.

Within a few minutes, the car had manoeuvred around a few blocks and found another parking space, nestling in behind a bright yellow Skoda, still keeping the front door of Madame Meatier's residence in direct sight.

*

It had taken Baxter a lot of persuasion to get his friend Brian at Fraud to hack into the County Council computer system. The guy owed him a favour after all, since he recommended his services on a previous job, but still he knew that an unsolicited intrusion into a government system was well out of his jurisdiction. He hoped that Brian was proficient enough to not only retrieve what he needed, but to leave no trace behind him. Eventually Rich had phoned him from the office saying that an unidentified email had come in, with an attachment of the entire contents of Trevor Hard's email inbox, and had he requested it? Naturally, Baxter denied it.

'OK, now you have got it, we might as well use it!' he had said, casually. 'Start with the most recent and see if you can find out where he is staying in France. Then text it to me. Oh, and Rich..?'

'Bax?'

'Don't mention it to the Boss!' The line went dead, but he was pretty sure his colleague wouldn't blow the whistle on him. Rich was a good cop who liked to keep his nose clean, but he would also be aware that Baxter would be promoted someday soon, and being on his side was a good place to be. Within 10 minutes, a text came through, with an address in La Rochelle.

'Cheers Bri, that's a pint I owe you,' he muttered out loud, turning the key of the Fiesta. His head had almost cleared now and he tried to recall the registration number on the lorry of the guy that lamped him one, but he didn't think he had it stored. All he could remember was that it was white and on Spanish plates, which could account for just about half the wagons on this stretch of the A16. That didn't stop him glancing up into the cab of each one that he passed. What he couldn't quite pinpoint was who was protecting Hard, and why? It was pretty obvious that someone knew he was following him, and that is why his car was blocked in; of that he was quite certain. It couldn't be coincidence could it? And that guy who whacked him, surely that was premeditated? Or was the driver just protecting his vehicle?

'I suppose he could have been?' he said out loud again, as his thoughts desperately searched around for evidence. Baxter checked his watch, it would be dark by the time he arrived at the town. His best plan would be to stay in the car and watch. Stake the place out for the evening, and follow Hard if he went out. That was assuming he hadn't already gone out and done the deal.

At 7.30pm he negotiated his small car along the crowded streets until he came to Rue du Temps. Parking spaces were hard to find, but it seemed that his suspect had managed to find one; there was no mistaking that glaring yellow estate car. It was Hard's alright, sitting there on its British number-plates. Then he considered the fact that he too was on British plates in this French town and would stick out like a sore thumb at a finger-puppet convention. Hurriedly he cruised along the street, omitting to notice two men, dressed in black, sitting in the car parked directly behind Hard's. They noticed him though.

'A contact, you think, Serge?' said one. Serge shrugged.

'I ain't paid to think!' he growled, his eyes following the Ford. 'You want me to check him out?'

'No!' snapped his partner, quickly. 'We wait, and we watch, and then we report. OK?' Again Serge shrugged and rubbed his knuckles.

*

'I'm Hard!' Try did his best to bow to the attractive woman as he was introduced.

'Alicia! Please to meet you Mister Hard.' He couldn't help being smitten by the woman's attractive features. Her cheek bones were so high that they framed her beautiful eyes in a shadow and her voice was gravelly and foreign, oozing with sex appeal. Alicia brushed her slender hand across the side of her cropped red hair as she smiled at him and Try's heart skipped so many beats, it was thumping out a reggae dub tune.

'This is my brother, Yashati.' Still focussed on her beautiful features, Try's heart suddenly raced forward like the hands of an over-wound watch.

'Yashati!' he exclaimed, turning to the man for the first time, his face forming an enormous smile.

'Wha's so funny? You laugh at my name?' Try had already offered his hand to shake and was now wishing he hadn't, as the man gripped it like a vice being tightened by an extremely strong wrestler.

'No!' he grimaced. 'Not at all. That's my name, too!'

'Your name is Yashati?' Yashati released the vice a couple of turns. 'Why didn't you say so? I am Albanian. From Albania,' he snarled. 'It is Albanian name!' His accent was strong, as though English was a struggle for him.

'My Mother!' replied Try weakly, shaking his now released hand which had turned purple. 'My Mother was from Albania.'

'Is good place, Albania! Better than this pigsty!' It wasn't the reaction Try had hoped for, and he backed away.

'Yashi, that's enough!' snapped the beautiful Alicia, indicating for Try to sit in the empty seat opposite. Yashi looked down to the plate of soup in front of him, like a puppy that had just been bashed with a copy of yesterday's newspaper.

As Try took his seat, Madame Meatier ladled a spoon of boiling brown liquid into a dish and set it down on the placemat. It had things floating in it. Try glanced to the other two dinner guests and smiled pathetically. They both nodded to him, their identical square glasses wobbling on their noses like a couple of street puppets.

'Gutten Tag!' They even spoke in unison. Try guessed they must be twins, or even clones! Turning his attention back to his soup, he did his best not to stare at the woman sitting opposite him, who was far and away the most beautiful woman he had ever set eyes on, let alone shared a table with. In order to take his mind from an un-invited erection rising under the table, Try quickly rearranged his cutlery into threes, moving his dessert spoon to replace the soup spoon he had just picked up. It was difficult habit to break. Yashi sucked at his spoon noisily, the sound piercing the awkward air like a like a hooting owl in an otherwise silent bell-tower. After a minute or so, the bell tolled, in the form of Madame Meatier.

'Monsieur 'Ard. When did you last come?'

Uncontrollably, Hard sprayed soup from the bowl of his spoon in a projectile, splashing on to Yashi's pristine white shirt. As if in slow motion, the Albanian first inspected the stain, and then raised his eyes towards Try. From the way his eyes narrowed and an evil scowl darkened across his face, you would have thought he had been shot, rather than just received spec of discolour on his clothes. Cowering back into his seat, Try was convinced the man was going to stand up and grab him round the throat, before Alicia put a steadying hand on his shoulder and offered him a napkin.

'To France, Monsieur? When did you last come to France?' explained Madame.

At first Try let out a slight giggle when he fully understood the question he had been innocently asked. Before he could help himself, the giggle turned to a short laugh which in turn swelled into a bigger laugh, freeing itself from within him like a steam valve after his long and eventful day. Unable to see the funny side, five other dinner participants studied the laughing man with a mixture of disdain and bewilderment, as though he was some sort of hyena. Try did his best to stop until he glanced up into the eyes of the flame-haired beauty in front of him, but then the look in her eyes, coupled with her suggestive smile set him off again, only this time, she joined in. When he turned to the confused Madame, his inner laughter only intensified until his shoulders were rising up and down in rhythm, until he had no idea what it was he was laughing at.

'I am glad I make you laugh, Monsieur,' said Madame, sternly. 'It is true that the Eenglish have a strange sense of humour. Do tell me what is so funny, so I can laugh too?'

Try just shook his head, unable to speak.

'You are a funny man,' laughed Alicia, waving her finger at him and shaking her own head. As she did so, her earrings jingled from side to side, bushing against her high cheek bones. Beneath her chin, the cleavage of two well-suntanned breasts nearly sent Try's brain dizzy with excitement as his laughter was abruptly exchanged for a gasp, his mouth remaining open like a bullfrog. With a realisation that he was staring again, he dragged his gaze away and back to the woman who was addressing him.

'Well?' she demanded.

'Errr. I am not sure you would understand, Madame Meatier.'

Not to be outdone by an Albanian youngster with film-star looks, the larger woman smiled a seductive smile at him.

'Call me Sylvie, please,' her tone softening to a purr, as her eyes bore into his. Suddenly, Try felt his excitement evaporate, as the excess of blood that had been heading towards his nether regions now rose up under his shirt collar with embarrassment.

'Never!' he blurted, trying to swallow a lump in his throat. 'This is my first time.'

'Aha.' She clapped her hands. 'I thought so. A virgin! I can always spot a virgin.' The woman's eyes held his gaze, daring him to break her stare. Desperately he wanted to gaze back to Alicia, but he hadn't the nerve. Eventually, she let his gaze go, and smiled. 'I can see I will 'ave to teach you!' With that, the obese woman pushed back her chair and stood up. 'And now! Some wine!' she laughed, reaching for a bottle on the sideboard. It was more of a statement than a question and before he could decline, a crystal glass in front of Try was filled to the brim.

Try wasn't really a wine man. He had never liked the taste of it since he had taken communion at school. In total, 6 boys had joined that Confirmation class at the age of 13, none for religious reasons. Try's motive was to get him out of rugby practice, whereas the others had just done it to get some free wine. As soon as the Chaplain's back was turned, they would scoot into the unlocked cupboard in the chapel, pour out most of the red wine from its bottle into an army water-bottle and replace it with a mixture of blackcurrant juice and vinegar. The boys would then take their booty to a den behind the bike sheds and pass it around. Try was never really invited into that circle, except one time, when the bottle he was passed did actually contain the horrid mixture. He had drunk a large swig and then been violently sick all over Bryan Gryffyths' Raleigh Chopper. And that had got him a beating, firstly from Bryan Gryffyths himself and then from his house-master who had been given the tip-off that the boys had been drinking alcohol.

No, Try was definitely not a wine drinker; half a weak lager was much more his style.

'Mesdames et Monsieurs,' shrieked the burly woman in her floral outfit, waving her glass in the air. 'A toast! To Les Anglais!' Both women, plus the two Germans, raised their glasses in Try's direction.

'Les Anglais!' they muttered in unison. Try was quite touched; he had never had a glass raised on his behalf before, especially by a woman with who he was falling in love with at first sight. To her right, he noticed that Yashi had not joined in the toast, choosing to gulp at his glass solemnly instead.

'Merci!' Try felt obliged to take a sip from his glass in response, letting the sharp red liquid flow down his throat. For all of his years of avoiding red wine, he decided this didn't actually taste as bad as he had expected.

'En France, we have the best wine in the whole world!' encouraged Sylvie, draining half of hers in one go. 'Les Anglais, they drink pees!'

'Pees?'

'Oui. You make wine that tastes like weewee!' The woman laughed again, loudly.

'I wouldn't know, I have never drunk any English wine.' Try was quite disturbed by the accusation, failing to join in the laughter. Realising her teasing was getting no response, Sylvie got up from the table and cleared away the soup plates, stopping at Try's shoulder and bending over to pour him some more wine. As she did this, she made a point of brushing her huge breast against the side of his face. Try instantly pulled back, repelled by the offending object. When Sylvie had left the room, Alicia spoke again.

'I think she likes you?'

'Me?' Try felt the blood rising to his face again. 'Likes me? Oh no, she is just being a good host!'

'You need to be careful. I think she wants to teach you some things,' she giggled. Try thought it was the sexiest giggle he had ever heard. The sort of giggle that women made during clandestine love-scenes in romantic films. Try's mind stayed on the love-scene a fraction too long and he suddenly felt a twinge below the table again. Flustered, he changed the subject.

'Are you on holiday?'

Alicia glanced very briefly at her brother before answering.

'Yes, of course. It is a nice place. A lovely place.' Her brother sniffed and raised his head. 'There are some lively bars and a beach,' she continued, 'we are having a great time. Aren't we, Yashi?' The man replied in a foreign language, his face scowling. Alicia answered him with a rapid sentence in the same language. Try thought she sounded even more beautiful when she spoke Albanian. 'But we have to leave tomorrow. It is so sad. We love it here!'

In the pit of his stomach, Try felt a huge pang of disappointment. Something inside him had suggested that this woman would be here all week and that he would have time to covet and seduce her, bit by bit. He had already convinced himself that by the end of the week, he would have made love to her at least 3 times. And now those hopes were dashed. Unless. Unless, he could conquer her tonight? Try picked up his glass and drained it in one go, in a bid to give him strength.

An opening door and the delicious odour of cooked food snapped him from his thoughts, as a smiling bulk of voluptuousness appeared like a tarantula into her web, carrying a large dish.

'You like to Pork, don't you, Monsieur?!'

6

Ludovic Broule had been in the French police force for nearly 30 years, man and boy, and you didn't spend 30 years in a police uniform without learning a thing or two. To be more precise, he hadn't always been in uniform, in fact he never really joined up for the uniform at all. During his early years, Ludovic had been a detective with the Police Nationale – or Sûreté Nationale as it had been known back then – living and working amongst the razzmatazz of the vibrant Paris city underworld. In hindsight, he would admit that it hadn't all been strictly honest way back then, and quite a few of the officers had taken bribes, him included. As the sordid 1970's evolved into a cleaner 1980's, investigations had been demanded, corruption uncovered and badges handed in. Being a conscientious young man, Broule had managed to keep himself distanced from the worst of the activities but it had still left an unworthy tarnish on the whole department and he had realised it was time to move on. With a marriage nearing its end and no real home or family life, Ludovic Broule had opted for a life on the road, astride a gleaming motorcycle, and transferred to the traffic department. That was pretty much where he had been ever since.

Although technically he was still based in Paris, in the winter he had an old converted barn out in the country near Rouen, where he would spend his spare time hunting animals. By summer, he enjoyed his weekends in a small apartment near the sea, where he could relax and watch the world go by slowly on foot instead of in cars at dangerous speeds.

Now, as he pulled off the motorway for the final time this week, Broule noticed the small car on British number plates that he had seen in the service station earlier. It had belonged to a wiry young man with cropped hair and an arrogant attitude. Once a detective, always a detective, thought Broule, smiling to himself. But there had been something strange, hadn't there? That was why the man stuck out in his mind amongst the hundreds of people he had seen and spoken to that day. The Englishman had been bleeding. He had also been having an argument with someone in the toilets and then acting suspicious when Broule walked in. Whilst whiling away his 15 minute break, Broule had also seen him checking out that yellow British car which again was suspicious. Suddenly he linked the two together. Yes, there had been that pathetic man in his yellow car, and a phone call with the most abusive language he had heard outside the Parisian red light district. Was this other English chap the one who had made the call?

Officer Broule shook his head again inside his helmet. Leave it, Ludo, you're not a detective now, and you are off duty. Don't get involved in other people's problems that don't concern you.

All the same, the little car was going in the same direction as he was, more or less, so it wouldn't hurt to keep an eye on it, would it. Dozily he tailed it from a distance through the streets, just out of curiosity, and was just about to turn off towards his own apartment when he spotted something that intrigued him. He wasn't the only one who spotted it, as he watched the little Ford slow down as it drove past the parked yellow Skoda on British number-plates. There was no mistaking that car; he didn't need to check his notebook to know it was the one he had pulled over earlier. Broule pulled the bike into a doorway and watched the little car turn down a side street, obviously looking for a parking space. Keeping in the shadows, he walked around the corner in time to see it coming round the block again, just as another car was pulling out from the kerb. The little Ford took its parking space but, as he waited, the driver didn't get out of the car, just sat there staring into space. In itself, this wasn't really a suspicious act, parking your car and sitting in it, but, coupled with other events, Broule had an idea that maybe something was going to develop here.

It wasn't his problem, he knew that. He should just phone his suspicions in to the local department and get them to check out the two English cars; or at the very least keep an eye on them. Instead, he went to his bike and rode the five minute journey back to his apartment, washed and showered, before deciding to head back into town on foot for a pizza in O'Malley's bar on Rue Du Temps. On his way back to town, over an hour later, now wearing casual jeans and a light windcheater, Ludovic Broule ambled past the Ford and glanced in to see its driver still in the seat with his eyes closed. Crossing the road, he checked the Skoda was still in the same place and was just heading to the restaurant when he noticed another car, on Paris number plates, parked directly behind it. It too had its inhabitants still in situ, both of them wearing dark clothes and one in sunglasses. Somehow, he felt that when he glanced at them, one of the men tried to slide down in his seat as if not wanting to be seen. A more villainous looking person was difficult to imagine. Whereas before he had been mildly suspicious that something might develop between the two Englishmen, he was now certain that here was an interesting situation just waiting to happen.

Waiting. That seemed the order of the evening. Ludovic managed to get a table by the window in the restaurant, where he could keep one eye on proceedings while casually reading the evening newspaper.

*

After his third large glass of wine, the world started to change for Trevor Richard Yashati Hard. For one thing, it occasionally went round a bit too quickly. For two, and far more importantly in his own mind, he had fallen head over heels in love with a woman with whom he desperately wanted to have sex. Under the table, a sensuous foot was working its toes around his inner ankle, something which had definitely never happened to him before and its efforts had raised his own manhood to attention. Above the table there was pleasant conversation and occasional laughter, as he tried to make pathetic conversation with someone who seemed like she was from another world. Even the way she ate her food oozed with sex appeal and, in his drunken mind, Hard felt the evening was going swimmingly well. Unfortunately, before he knew it, swimming was what was happening on the table, as a Madame Metier accidentally knocked over a whole bottle of Chateau Brise d'Armiet 2007 – Try distinctly noticed the label as it fell - which then cascaded down onto Alicia's lap. To say this put quite a dampener on the evening would be a cliché. With the speed and grace of a Thomson Gazelle, the Albanian beauty was on her feet and dashing from the room amidst a flurry of foreign swearwords Try was quite glad he did not understand. So desperately he wanted to dash after her, to help her out of her wet clothes and then ravish her as she stood naked before him. But before he had enough courage to stand to his feet, Yashi had pushed his chair back and beaten him to it.

'Idiot!' he snarled to Madame.

'Oops,' she replied, making no attempt to clean up the mess. In a blur of confusion, Try turned towards her, to be greeted by a smile that included the tip of a suggestive tongue between the teeth. It was at this very point that he realised his ankle was still being caressed by a fine set of toes. In fact they no longer remained on his ankle, but were climbing up his inner thigh at a quite alarming rate and rubbing at his semi-erect anatomy.

'Bu..but!' objected his drunken voice. 'The.. table?' Before he could protest further, like an alien predator, Sylvie leapt from her chair, wrapped her arms around him and engulfed his still moving mouth in a suffocating kiss that would have fetched a fatally wounded soldier back to life. Flailing his arms like a seventies disco dancer, Try did his utmost to resist this creature who was about to suck out his fillings.

'The table, yes, yes..!' she screeched, allowing him chance to momentarily refill his lungs with air, 'Sur le tableau, maintenant!!'

Almost bodily dragging the poor man to his feet, Madame Meatier – pronounced Met-i-air - simultaneously slammed the door shut with one foot, grabbed at his rapidly diminishing crutch with one hand while releasing two buttons from the front of her brightly coloured floral frock with the other. It has to be said, it was a movement so fast and impressive that Jackie Chan himself would have been proud of it, especially as it was made by someone three times his size. Faced directly with two of the largest organs any man could imagine in his wildest dreams, Try gave the biggest struggle of his life, even bigger than when Bryan Gryffyths' pals had held him down for a beating, but to no avail. Sylvie's giant naked bazookas thrust towards him with the force of a scrap-yard car-crusher, as he was pinned back on to the table like an overpowered wrestler. In the final moment while his lungs were still full of air, Try did the only decent thing that any upstanding member of the male community would have done in such a situation. He screamed!

*

Napoleon was not like any ordinary dog. His was a demented world, where sounds and smells came and went, while he spent much of his time locked away from it all. In a previous life he had been out on the Chasse, nimbly picking his way through the woods chasing, catching and brutally tearing apart his prey. From an early age, his master had trained him to come hither by means of a whistle. He had hated it, but he had also never forgotten it. Like Pavlov's experimental creatures of years ago, when Napoleon heard a whistle, he basically went ape-shit.

Since those early years, he had escaped one day, ended up in a Rescue Home, fought with the majority of the other occupants including the humans, and been listed for death by lethal injection. By a stoke of luck, - and as Charles Manson would be the first to point out, on death row, any sort of luck is good luck - Madame Meatier had walked in through the door that very day. Napoleon had liked this large smiling woman and she had been ultra-kind to him up to the point when she had his testicles removed. To be fair, she had this done for a fairly good reason and not without warning, because Napoleon had developed a nasty habit of trying to hump the guests, which was possibly something he had learned from his new owner. Since the operation his sexual tendencies had waned slightly but he still enjoyed a good romp with anyone prepared to play, and often even if they weren't, when he was let loose amongst human beings. Thankfully, this wasn't frequently.

To all intents and purposes, you could say that, after nearly three years under the masterful ownership of Sylvie Meatier, Napoleon was almost a normal dog - except when certain sounds disturbed him. One of those sounds was that of men screaming, of anyone screaming in fact, which triggered off dark images from his past, and caused him to get rather angry. Another sound that set him off was the telephone ringing, which reminded him, somewhere in his deranged dog-brain of a whistle.

It was ringing now, although the sound of it ringing in the household could barely be heard above the din that Napoleon was making, as he barked, howled, spun in circles and threw himself at the locked door. His noise also drowned out that of the man screaming. Having stayed in the house for three days already, Alicia was aware of the issues that a ringing telephone caused to the dog and scurried from her room, in a state of half undress, to answer it.

'Allo!'

'Mrs Meatier?'

'Er, no. I think she is busy...!'

A crash of plates from within the dining room confirmed that she was indeed busy.

'Pardon. You'll have to shout. It's a bit noisy in here,' continued Alicia in a loud voice, still buttoning up her jeans. Napoleon had quietened down a little, but was still hurling himself at the door which was starting to give.

'Mr Hard. Yes he is here. But I think he is busy too!' Alicia smiled to herself, for a second, but then the smile dropped from her face. 'Oh. Yes. If it's important.' She propped the receiver against the hall table and padded over to the dining room door in her bare feet, listened for a second and then knocked.

'Mr Hard. You have a phone call,' she shouted. 'It's the Police!'

In wrestling or boxing, or other sports of a similar barbaric nature, this moment could be referred to as 'being saved by the bell'! Behind the door, the sport of another barbaric nature being administered by Madame Meatier ceased long enough for Try to spring from her clutches and make it to the door, wrenching it open to see the backside of the lovely Alicia scurrying back towards her room. It was a welcome sight to a drunken man who was rapidly sobering up. Try gulped in some air, dashed from the room and slammed the door behind him. If there had been a key, he would have locked it, to contain the beast inside, and then perhaps thrown it away, or even swallowed it. As he headed to the telephone, he caught sight of himself in the hall mirror to see his face was so covered in red lipstick that he looked as though he had been in a car crash. Frantically wiping it from his face, Try considered that a car crash, even a fatal one, would have been a far more pleasing experience than the ordeal he had just endured.

'Hello!' he shouted, above the noise of Napoleon. 'It's Hard here! It's hard to hear.' At the door of her room, and the door of the room next door, two Albanian ears agreed that it was indeed hard to hear, as they tried their best to listen in on the conversation.

'Suspects? Oh...' He pushed the phone tight to his ear, listening to the questions.

'Yes. Two of them....' Listening again.

'Max Hornsby? No. No idea....' More listening.

'Yashati? Yes. Albanian.... Okay. Goodbye officer.'

Behind the door in room number 5, this phone call had come as very bad news indeed, where its occupant had gone quite pale. The same could be said for room number 6. The police. Suspect. Two of them. Albanain. Max Hornsby. Every one of these words were bad news.

Try was just running the conversation through his mind.

There had been a crime in Birmingham and the police were just checking out a few suspects.

Had he had a phone call from a stranger with a gruff abusive voice? Yes, he had two of them.

Did he know Max Hornsby? No. Why had he been phoning him? No idea.

His middle name, Yashati, was that Eastern European? Yes. Albanian.

Try was just considering what strange questions these were when behind yet another door, after one last effort, the latch gave way unleashing a creature looking for action. At that very same moment, in a bid to get some fresh air in his lungs, Try had coincidentally opened the front door. Napoleon flew across the hall like an Excocet missile aimed at the man whose voice he had recently heard screaming. Fortunately for him, said man sidestepped like a seasoned toreador, and the deranged creature flew through the front door and out on to the street. Before it had chance to make a u-turn, Try slammed the door again.

The inside of his head was going around like a Hotpoint washing machine on full spin cycle. So many things were happening at once, that a sane and sober person would have been on the very edge of their capacity to comprehend the situation. To a drunken, love-struck, abused, suspected and exhausted simpleton such as Trevor Hard, the world had become so confusing, he might as well be playing Suduko, in Chinese! To top it all, the door to the dining room was opening and from it was emerging the worst of all his nightmares.

Try dived into his bedroom, locked the door, wedged a wooden chair under the handle, lay on his bed and passed out.

7

By 9.30 in the evening, things in the Rue du Temps were starting to hot up. Baxter Collins had been awoken from his light sleep by screaming coming from the house of Madame Meatier. This had caused him to emerge from his vehicle in order to get a little closer to the action. In a hopeful attempt to see what was going on inside the house, he had crossed the street, crept up the front steps and put his eye to the keyhole, only to be faced with a vision of loveliness, pulling on skin-tight jeans over skimpy underwear while answering the telephone in a foreign accent. She had then run away, and his suspect, Trevor Hard, had come to the phone. Baxter hadn't managed to hear the conversation as a pedestrian had walked past, so he had to pretend he was just reading the room-rates on the plaque outside the door. As soon as the passing man had gone, the drug-squad officer was just putting his eye to the door again when it opened and he was bowled over by something resembling the Hound of the Baskervilles which was moving at 100 miles per hour. Whilst he was on the ground, the manic creature had then licked at his face with such a force that it removed the false moustache he had been wearing as a disguise, whist simultaneously gripping him around the torso and humping him for all it was worth. Completely helpless to remove the offending creature, Baxter was desperately fumbling around his jacket for his gun when a loud whistle stopped the creature in its tracks. Behind him, a tall man with a greying moustache blew three short blasts causing the dog to change its state of mind from sexually active to intense anger. Leaving its previous prey in a compromised position on the pavement, Napoleon then made a move that he was to regret for the rest of his life. In actual fact, the rest of his life was not very long at all. Officer Broule's first shot hit the air-born creature directly in the chest and a second one followed it in rapid succession. By the time the animal landed it was a dead as a Tuesday night out in Brighton.

Within a few seconds, a door above him opened and in its frame appeared the gigantic figure of Madame Meatier herself, who looked down on the situation and saw Baxter Collins scrambling to his feet, holding a gun, while her beloved dog lay lifeless on the pavement. Before Baxter had time to proclaim his innocence, she was already bearing down on him with both fists, screaming like a banshee. For the second time in as many minutes, he was once again rendered helpless until other forces came to his rescue. This time it took a little longer.

In a dimly lit car which was parked adjacent to the proceedings, Serge – or Batman, as his friend had just referred to him – watched this fierce woman beating the crap out of a defenceless passer-by with one eyebrow raised. When his partner gave him a nudge, he just raised his eyebrow even further.

'Well, go on then..!' the man demanded.

'But, it's a woman!'

'I can see it's a woman!'

'I ain't getting involved with no woman..'

'Well, if you don't stop her, there will be a murder.'

Serge shook his head and his partner was just about to open the door and sort out the situation himself, when he stopped and slunk back down into his seat.

Outside on the pavement, Madame Meatier's victim was screaming so loudly that the noise was echoing up the narrow street and mingling with the assorted sounds of disco beats coming from a few club doorways. Very shortly the sound was complimented by that of a police siren, as a pair of gendarmes in a blue striped car screeched to a halt. Within seconds, two pairs of handcuffs were administered, as a crowd of onlookers gathered round to watch, amidst a flurry of swearing in two languages. Ludovic stood well back from the incident that he had just reported by an anonymous phone call, leaving the locals to ably do their job. Both Baxter and the struggling homicidal woman, along with the body of a large dog, were instantly shoved into the back of the police car which headed off towards the main station, leaving a street full of bewildered onlookers in its wake.

As the car drove away, Ludovic noticed a face peering out from behind the curtain in the guest house, that of a man with dark features and black wavy hair.

Inside the hallway of the house, now that the police-car had taken away its proprietor, two Albanians were having a heated argument. In Albanian. Loosely translated, it went as follows.

'I don't know, Yashi. I don't know why he spoke to the police. I don't even know who he is.' Alicia's voice was shrill when she yelled.

'But this has messed everything up. First he talks to the police about 2 Albanians, then that woman gets taken for questioning. Don't you see? They are on to us!'

'They are not on to us, Yashi. Just stay calm. It is a coincidence! OK?'

'No. Not OK.' The foreign man repeatedly ran his hands though his hair. 'Not OK. We screw this up, we are finished. And we are so close now. Just one more night.'

Out in the street, Ludovic stood in the shadows, considering what might be going on, as the noise of the argument spilled out under the door. In the car parked outside, 2 men dressed in black were doing something similar. Behind a locked door in bedroom number 3, one half-drunken, half-terrified, half-witted, love-struck man stirred from his sleep, awaking to the sound of the girl of his dreams, shrieking, in Albanian. Try clutched on to the sides of the bed, to stop it spinning round. It didn't help. As the shouting continued, the contents of his stomach started to spin too and a familiar tremor rose slowly up through his gullet. Disorientated and confused, he made a gallant attempt to clamber to his feet, tripping over the chair against the door, and threw up into a waste-paper basket with a groan.

'Shhh. He's awake,' whispered Alicia, pointing to the bedroom door.

'The bastard!' whispered her brother. 'He's been listening to us. He speaks Albanian. He's a fucking spy. I'll have to kill him.'

'Shh!' she said again. 'I'll deal with him. You go and phone Max. See if we can go tonight.' Alicia gave the man a glare of authority and he retreated. 'Tonight,' she repeated.

*

'He killed my Nappy..!' wailed the woman from the back seat of the car, in French. 'He shot him. Poor defenceless Napoleon. He shot him!' For the tenth time, Sylvie tried to attack Baxter who cowered in the corner of the seat.

'That woman's a lunatic. Get her away from me!' he yelled. 'You can't arrest me. I am the police!' In the front seat the driver rolled his eyes. A violent woman beating up a man for killing her dog? The man claiming he is the police. Just a usual domestic incident for a Friday night.

'Not 'ere, you are not, Monsieur. I 'ave told you. You might be policeman in Eeengland. But ere, you are not allowed to go round shooting dogs.' The man shook his head as Baxter protested.

'But I didn't kill the dog!'

'Yes you did, you murderer. You dog murderer!' Again the woman struggled and Baxter hoped the handcuffs would hold out.

'You can tell your stories to the Sergeant,' said the other policeman, as the car pulled to a halt outside the station and he opened the door.

Inside the police station, a desk sergeant completed a long and complicated form, taking details from both of them, all the while Baxter protesting that he was a police officer and demanding his right to a phone call. Every time he spoke, Sylvie spat at him venomously.

'You Eeenglish pig. You dog murdering pig!' Eventually Baxter was taken to an interview room, pushed roughly down onto a chair and the door locked behind him. There he waited for almost an hour before anyone else arrived and a further 25 minutes before he was released without charge after it was confirmed that his weapon had not been fired for a few weeks. Dejected and exhausted, Baxter Collins stepped out into the balmy night to continue his quest to snare Trevor Hard.

*

Meanwhile, in a small bedroom on Rue du Temps, an Albanian temptress with flame-red hair had beaten him to it.

At first Try had been reluctant to open the bedroom door when he heard the gentle tap.

'Mister Hard, are you OK in there? You sound unwell?' He was indeed unwell but, somewhere in his fuzzy brain, the soft words of this Albanian beauty struck a sweet note. 'You poor man. Why don't you open the door and let Alicia take care of you.' For a few seconds, Try lifted his head from the bin until it started to swirl again and he hung on to the wall. Was this really happening? Unsteadily he pushed the chair aside and turned the handle, pulling the door open a fraction. With his eye to the small crack, he peered through it like a small boy peeping out from under the bed covers. When he saw Alicia standing there alone, he pulled the door wider.

'Mister Hard,' she purred again, 'are you alright?'

'Huh? Oh, yes, I am fine,' he stuttered, wiping his mouth on his sleeve. For a second Alicia stood back, before stepping forward and pushing the door.

'Can I come in?' Try felt his knees start to tremble as a seductive smile widened across the woman's face.

'*It's her! It's her!!*' shouted out a voice in his head.

'Well?'

'Errr, yes please. Yes. Please do.' Alicia stepped inside and sat on the bed, while Try closed the door behind her, the sweet smell of her perfume filling the room and slightly disguising the smell of vomit. When she patted the bed for him to sit down next to her, he once again resisted the urge to look behind him in case she was beckoning someone else.

'It is my last night in France,' she continued, 'and I wanted to get to know you better.' Try's world tried to focus. 'I don't even know your first name. You do have a first name, don't you Mister Hard?' Moving her face close to his ear, she moved one hand down onto his leg. 'Or should I just call you Hard?'

'T..t..Try!' he blurted out.

'Try? I am trying, Mister Hard,' replied the girl without missing a beat. Her hand delved slightly nearer to his crotch as her lips brushed his ear. On his neck he could feel the warmth of her breath as she whispered a sentence to him in Albanian.

'Dear mother of god!' he replied as his knee started to shake.

'No. That wasn't the right answer!' She cupped her hand over his bulging crotch and whispered the words again, so sensually he felt every hair on his body rise up. By the tone of the voice, it was a question.

'Yes. Yes please…!' he replied. Alicia removed her hand and sat upright, a big smile spreading on her face.

'You don't understand, do you?'

'Err, yes I do,' said Try desperately. 'I want you.'

'But I asked you a question and you didn't know the answer.'

'Err, no. Yes. I will do whatever you say.' In his world of confusion, he realised he was shaking uncontrollably. 'I didn't quite hear you.'

'I asked you…' she stood to her feet. 'I asked you, if you wanted me to leave now?' Turning her slender body towards the door, she spoke to him over her shoulder. 'You don't speak Albanian, do you Mister Hard?'

'Try..' he replied feebly. 'It's Try. No I don't.' The woman was already opening the door as he pleaded. 'Please don't go..!'

'Oh,' she stopped. 'One more question..?'

'Yes. Anything. I'll do anything.'

'What did the police want?' Alicia stepped back into the room, closing the door behind her again. This time she stayed on her feet, the smile falling from her face as her eyes narrowed. 'Who are you really, Mister Hard?' Alicia raised her slender leg and pushed a stiletto heel into the place where her hand had recently been. 'Why do you talk to the police, Mister Hard!'

'I don't know?'

'You don't know who you are?'

'Yes. No. I..I don't know what the police wanted. Something about a murder..!'

'A murder? You are not a murderer, are you, Mister Hard?'

'No..!' he almost shouted the words as the heel of the shoe pressed a bit harder.

'Good.' Alicia stood for a second thinking. 'What did you tell to Sylvie, Mister Hard? What did you tell her, that she can tell the police?' Try looked up at her pathetically, still marvelling at her beauty despite now being so petrified that any minute he thought his bladder would let him down.

'Nothing. I didn't tell her nothing! Anything!' His mind raced back to an hour earlier when that huge woman had thrust her breasts at him and his stomach started to churn. Alicia noticed the paleness rising in his face and stepped back, indicating towards the bathroom.

'Good. Then we have nothing to worry about, do we?' With that Try dived into the tiny bathroom, slamming the door behind him. Alicia rolled her eyes, as she heard the groaning sounds of him vomiting behind the door. Satisfied that she had succeeded in her task, she picked up his wallet from the side table, retrieved the key from the inside lock on the bedroom door, left the room and locked it from the outside.

8

'That's them!' Serge jumped in his seat as the man dug him in the ribs, waking up with a start.

'Will ya stop doing that!' he snapped, looking out through the steamed window to see two people leaving through the front door of the town house. He ran his hand across the front of his stubbly chin. 'You want me to whack em?'

'No, Serge. We follow them. Right? Nobody whacks anybody!' Serge looked a little disappointed.

'Bit of a looker, though, ain't she?'

'If they split up, you take him and I will follow her.'

'How come you get's the girl?'

'Because he looks dangerous! And you like danger, don't you Serge?'

Serge said nothing for a minute, just watched his prey as they headed up the street.

'When do I get to whack im, then?' His partner was already opening the door, indicating him to do the same.

'Come on, Batman,' he sighed quietly. 'Let's just do what we're paid to do.'

In a seat by the window in O'Malleys café, Ludovic pulled the newspaper a bit higher to hide his face, as first a foreign looking couple walked past, and then two slightly more shady looking gentlemen dressed in black followed them a few hundred yards behind. The officer folded up his paper, left a twenty euro note on the table and stepped out into the fresh air of the crowded street.

Minutes later, a blue-striped squad car once again pulled up on Rue Du Temps, unloading a large angry woman from the back seat who had been released without charge. Once Sylvie Meatier had recovered from the shock of losing her dog, she was secretly quite glad. The immense beast had been a liability from the first day she had him, and his antics, particularly his sexual tenancies towards other humans, had not been good for business. In fact she had recently posted an advert in a local paper to find him a new home, but had only had one taker, a frail man in his seventies who was levelled to the floor within seconds of their first introduction. Her only other option would have been to have him put down, and now that had been done for her. The only real concern she had was that the Englishman had been released as there was no evidence that he had fired a shot from his gun. If he hadn't done it, then just who had? That's what she wanted to know. That was what the police wanted to know too. While she was contemplating this, she opened the front door to her own house, thankful that it was unlocked as she had no key with her, and was just heading to the bathroom when she heard someone thumping on one of the bedroom doors. He was shouting too, in English.

'Let me out, please. I think I love you!'

Of course, thought Sylvie, the little Englishman. He wasn't much to look at, but he had potential and she was doing rather well with him until the fracas with the dog had interrupted things. And now here he was declaring his love for her. Madame Meatier stepped lightly across the parquet floor to her own personal bathroom and freshened herself up, ready for round two.

Behind the door, Try was anything but fresh. His mouth was dry, and his trousers wet. Blood dripped from his knuckles, where he had spent the last 10 minutes hammering on the door in a continuous frenzy, as the alcohol in his system drove him on towards a sexual fantasy. For much of his life, Try had often gotten the wrong end of the stick, something which invariably got him into situations beyond his comprehension. This was definitely one of those occasions. After the woman of his desires had left the room earlier, Try had considered that she had been teasing him and that furthermore, she would return any minute to carry on with her games which would possibly evolve into passionate sex. Although he was slightly bemused by her questions about the police, the poor chap was genuinely convinced that this Albanian beauty desired him just as much as he desired her and that maybe she had gone to change into a fake police uniform. When he heard the front door opening and footsteps in the hallway, he was pretty sure it was her returning.

'Let me out. I love you!'

Sylvie turned the key quietly in the door lock.

'Ere I am, Mon Cherie. Sylvie's here now,' she crooned, pushing the door inwards. 'I love you too, my little pamplemoose!'

Not for the first time that evening, screams could be heard out in the Rue du Temps. Not for the first time, the screams were witnessed by a member of the British police force as Baxter Collins arrived outside the front door. Not for the first time, the front door opened and something came out through it at near 100 miles per hour, bowling him back down to the street. Deja-vu is often a frightening thing, especially if it features a gigantic woman looking fearfully down from an open doorway while you are lying on the floor at her mercy. The fact that this woman has already tried to kill you several times in the last few hours only helps to make the matter worse. As Trevor Hard sprinted up the street in a gallant attempt to escape this rampant woman, so Baxter jumped to his feet and headed after him as fast as his feet would travel, driven on by fear and desperation in equal measures. Behind him, the woman shouted a mixture of obscenities and niceties, all in very colourful French, before closing the door and locking it.

Try had no idea where he was running, as he buffeted his way through crowds of people in the narrow street. Once or twice, as he glanced back, he sure he was being followed which only persuaded him to quicken his pace. Had his mind considered that his pursuer was supposedly a large woman in a flowing floral dress and breasts the size of zeppelins, it may have wondered how come the creature could move after him so athletically. However, bearing the fact that his mind had been through so many wringers in the last few hours that it was now mangled well beyond the ability to produce rational thoughts of its own, his legs were doing all the thinking instead. Towards the top of the narrow street was a blue sign depicting a small boat, directing people towards the Port. His legs took this route - possibly considering that they may at some stage be able to swim away from this danger - of their own accord. Ahead of him the street widened slightly, enabling his passage down the hill to become a bit easier. Easier it may have been for a sober rational man with a reasonable sense of balance. As Try was none of these things, he soon found himself tumbling, crashing into one tourist after another. Pretty soon there were no more tourists, as the waves parted before him and Try found himself cascading down onto the cobbled stones, head first.

*

Out in the harbour the dull drone of a foghorn cut through the night air, signalling that a cargo ship was coming into dock. Within minutes its great bulk loomed through the spotlights while the captain skilfully manoeuvred the massive steel hull into position amongst rows of cranes, as teams of dock-workers went about their routine tasks. Searchlights swung around in the sky and engines burst into life at the very instant that it clanked to standstill against the quayside. Ships like this one came in and out of the Bay of Biscay two or three times per day, each one carrying its own cargo, stacked in large steel containers. On the quay and on the first deck, men with clipboards scurried around while the overhead cranes started to swing, clanking their hooks on to one container at a time and swirling them slowly through the air. Each container bore huge letters and numbers on its side and every one was ticked off by Customs officials as it got stacked on the shore.

From a first floor apartment window, Alicia patiently watched the swinging boxes though a small set of binoculars, checking the numbers against the piece of paper in her hand.

*

Baxter stood over the body lying on the stones as, once again, a small crowd of tourists gathered around, mumbling to each other. Who was this deranged man? Why had he been running like an out of control whirling dervish? Bending down, Baxter checked for a pulse in his neck. Hard was still alive.

'It's alright. Stand back. I am a doctor!' he announced to whoever was listening. 'That wasn't very clever, old chum, was it?' he whispered near Try's unconscious ear. 'Now what do we do, eh?' Effortlessly, he rolled the body over on to its back, checking a scar on Try's forehead. It was nothing too serious; the man would live. But he wasn't going to make a pick-up, lying here unconscious, was he? And by the speed he had been running, the pick-up time must be pretty soon. To the dismay of one or two of the gathered crowd, Baxter grasped Try under the arms and dragged him to the side of the street, propping him up against a stone wall.

'Urrrghh!' said the body.

'That's better, mate, you come on round so we can see what you're up to?'

'Meatier..!'

'Meteor?' repeated Baxter. Must be a code name of some sort, he thought. Maybe the name of the contact? Or the whole operation. Yes, Operation Meteor, that sounded familiar. In the distance at the bottom of the street, Baxter could make out glinting water in the harbour and hear the sounds of boats and workers.

'Albanian..!' said the delusional mind of Try Hard, as his brain struggled to bring itself back to the land of the living.

'Albanian?' repeated the drug-squad officer, as though making a mental note. 'Come on pal, what else you got to tell me?' Baxter gave him a slap across the face with the palm of his hand. 'Tell me more..,' he said, raising his voice. He slapped him again, a bit harder and Try fell sideways. Then a thought crossed Baxter's mind. What if he had made the pick-up already? Instantly, he ran his hands around Try's pockets, feeling for any packages.

'He's hitting him!' shouted a young woman who had been watching the proceedings. 'And now he's robbing him!'

'Oy, get off him, you, or I'll call the police!' Baxter glanced up at the girl and snarled at the spotty youth by her side.

'Piss off and mind you own business!'

'Help...!' mumbled Try feebly.

'Look! Someone help. This thug has beaten up a poor defenceless guy, and now he's robbing him.' The English woman was already running to get help. She found it in the shape of a giant man with a scarred face and hands like loading-shovels who was lurking in the shadows of a doorway nearby. The man lumbered across the street and looked down at Baxter, who was still sorting through Try's pockets.

The next thing Baxter Collins knew was that he was being lifted through the air by his jacket collar. Using his police-trained self defence, he swung his fist directly into the giant man's face, connecting with his rough cheek. It was a punch that would have floored most criminals. But Serge wasn't like most criminals. He shook his head slowly and grinned at Baxter, revealing one silver tooth. That was the last thing Baxter remembered.

Meanwhile, Try was starting to come to his senses - or what little senses he had amassed in his 40 or so years - and opened his eyes. Above him in the near darkness loomed a hulk of a man whom, despite his best efforts at trying to focus, he did not recognise. His first thoughts were that of relief. At least it wasn't a 15 stone voluptuous woman in a floral dress. Raising one arm, he touched a lump on the top of his head, feeling sticky warmth oozing from it. Blood. Try wasn't good with blood, especially when it was his own, so his mind, now considering taking charge of his body once again, decided to shut down again. As his eyes closed a blurred vision of an Albanian beauty floated happily somewhere behind his eyelids. Yes things certainly seemed better with them closed. In the next instant, he was rising to his feet and almost walking. Except his feet weren't really supporting him and he was sort of floating along.

During his simple life, Try had watched one or two films and his favourite one had been one called 'Ghost'. He had seen it a dozen times. In it, Patrick Swayzee gets killed in a street fight, but his ghost rises up and starts running around trying to get the guy who did it to him. It also stars a beautiful woman. In Try's semi-conscious mind, he was in that film right now. Quickly his eyes flashed open, glanced down at the ground moving under his feet and then saw a lifeless body lying on the ground behind him. Yep, that was enough to convince him that he was positively dead. Any minute now, some music would start playing but he couldn't remember what it was. Not being one to leave out details such as this, his mind delved around amongst the memory banks, looking for the track like an old Wurlitzer jukebox as he floated a few hundred yards down the street.

'Come on, it must be in there somewhere. Put some more money in..,' suggested the logical part of his brain.

In front of him, a door opened. He didn't see it open, just sensed it as he went through it and it closed behind him. Then he was sitting on a chair. Could this be the scene with the potter's wheel? Somewhere above him, there was light. If he was really dead, then maybe he could take a look at the light. What harm could it do. Try opened one eye.

'Good evening, Mister Hard,' said a deep voice. Try closed it again. 'Maybe you have something to tell us..hmm?' Try opened the other eye and looked up at the voice, it definitely wasn't Demi Moore.

'The Righteous Brothers?' he said.

A look of confusion came over the man's face before it broke into a hollow laugh. When Try's eyes managed to focus a little more in the bright light, he realised there was another man there too, and their combined laughter echoed around the room.

'Did you hear that, Serge? He thinks we are the Righteous Brothers!' Serge laughed so much it turned into a raspy cough as he bent over double. Who were these people? They shouldn't be in his dream. But one thing was for sure, if he was dead, they couldn't hurt him. Or had they hurt him already? Was this the man who had killed him? Instinctively, Try raised his hand to the bump on his head. Except he couldn't, because his arm wouldn't move. Then another thought crossed his mind, a more logical one. Well, logical to a confused man, who thinks he is dead.

'You're God, aren't you?' The men burst out laughing again. 'And he is Saint Peter?'

It was nearly a full minute before the men re-gathered their composure enough to answer.

'Nah, he ain't Saint Peter, he's Batman!'

Try closed his eyes again, hoping that when he opened them, Demi Moore would be there or, even better, Alicia. She wasn't. Nor Bruce Wayne.

'Where am I?' he sighed.

*

Baxter woke up thinking the same thing. Whoever - or whatever - had hit him had done it pretty hard. This day wasn't going well. One by one he tried to move his aching limbs, which all seemed intact. Then he reached into his pocket for his mobile phone. Maybe it was time to give the local police a call, perhaps they would be a bit more sympathetic this time. But his day got worse when he found that his pockets were empty. Not just his phone was missing, but his wallet and passport as well as his police badge.

Looking like some sort of tramp, he got himself to his feet and staggered out into the main street, clinging on to the wall for balance. Party-goers and tourists still filled the town, some of them now staggering themselves. In fact, he fitted right in. One man spoke to him in Spanish and Baxter tried to reply but he mouth was so dry the words wouldn't come out. He needed a drink of water, or perhaps something stronger, to help him organise his thoughts. At the top of the cobbled street, in the crowded square, was a small drinking fountain, where cool water spurted in the air from a little tap. Pushing his way through the crowd, Baxter stuck his head over it, gulping it down and then scooping it over his head and running his hands through his matted hair. For a minute or two, the liquid ran red as the worst of the blood washed away. One or two onlookers stood back when they saw this.

'You alright, pal?' asked one in a Glaswegian accent. Baxter said nothing. His mind was now trying to piece together what might have happened. It was obvious Hard was running towards his pick-up point, when maybe he had tripped. Or had someone hit him too? Obviously the man who had hit Baxter must have been the contact. One thing was pretty certain, if Hard and his gang were bringing drugs into the country, the shipment would come by sea. Shaking his head one more time, his mind focussed again. He needed to get back down to the harbour, and quick. He may also need some back-up.

*

'Arrrrggghhh!' screamed Try, as the man grabbed him even tighter in the crutch. 'I don't know who they are. They said they were just tourists.'

'But you are an Albanian, Mister Hard. You must have heard what they were saying?' The man nodded to Serge, who squeezed again.

'I…I..can't speak Albanian!' Sweat poured down his forehead as the excruciating pain increased. 'I wanted to have sex and they are leaving tomorrow!'

'Leaving tomorrow? Serge, I think you had better leave Mr Hard with enough equipment. He wants to have sex!' The big man smiled, revealing his silver tooth again, and then relieved the pressure.

'Why are you being followed by the police, Mister Hard?' continued the interrogator, changing tack. Try thought about this for a second or two.

'I don't think I am being followed. I just had a phone call from them, that's all.'

'A phone call?'

'Yes, they were investigating a murder.'

'A murder?'

'In Birmingham.' The man looked at Serge inquisitively for a moment, and then back to Try again.

'Did they give you a name?'

'No, they just said there had been a murder.'

'So why did they call you. Did you do the murder, Mister Hard?'

'I don't know!'

'You don't know if you did the murder? Are you sure? I think if you had done a murder, you would know?'

'No!'

'No, you don't know? Or no you didn't do it?'

'I didn't murder anyone!' his pitch went up an octave again as he felt the big hand starting to squeeze once more. 'They said his name was Max…arrggghh.' At that, the man held up his hand, thinking for a minute.

'Who's name was Max?'

'Max. Max's name was Max.'

'Max who?'

'I   can't   remember…………arrgghh! Humby…Handy…Horny..!'

'Hornsby?'

'Yes. Yes! Yes, that's him…!' Serge stopped squeezing again.

'I see.' The man shrugged. 'What do you think, Serge?'

'I ain't paid to think,' grunted the giant. Try focussed on his interrogator, in his suit and black tie. The voice sounded English, but with hint of foreign.

'Who are you?' he asked, timidly. The man laughed.

'I ask the questions here,' he snapped. 'But being as you ask, this here is Serge. He likes to hurt people. You can just call me…' the man thought for a second, rubbing his chin. 'K!' He rubbed his chin some more. 'Yes, K, that's my name.'

'How do you spell it?'

'What do you mean, how do you spell it. You don't spell it! It's just K.'

'Is it short for something? Like Kevin or something...Keith maybe?' K jumped forward, grinding his teeth.

'Shut-up, you fuck-wit, or Serge will rip your balls off and push them in your mouth. Do you understand? Now why was a fucking English policeman following you in a French town and going through your pockets.' By this point, Try was screaming very loudly.

'I don't know any English policeman. I haven't done anything..!' he wailed. Serge stood up to his full height.

'Whoa..take it easy, pal.'

'You're telling me to take it easy?! You? The fucking caped crusader? This fucking idiot is just wasting my time, and I am running out of patience.' K was yelling now, so he could be heard above the noise of Try who was screaming at the top of his voice, despite the fact that Serge was nowhere near him.

'What you want me to do with him?' asked the giant thug. 'You wanna me to kill him, maybe. Chuck him in the sea?' Try's screaming got even louder.

'We don't kill people, Serge,' shouted K, 'unless we're told to. Just tie him up and leave him here! Someone will find him eventually. We had better go and check on the other two.' Serge looked a bit disappointed.

'Whadda you want me to do with these?' he asked, holding up a wallet, mobile phone and police badge.

'Just chuck em in here with this idiot,' replied K, opening the door to the street. 'And shut the fucker up?' Within a few seconds, the screaming stopped, as Try slumped back down in his chair, unconscious again.

*

From her vantage point on the small first floor balcony, Alicia could see pretty much all of the harbour, as well as the busy dock workers scurrying about. Over in the lorry park, queues of wagons waited patiently for containers to be loaded, their drivers sitting in their cabs. Alicia could see one in particular, with a dark haired driver now wearing plain green overalls.

'Still no sign of it, just be patient!' she said quietly into her mobile phone.

'It should be 'ere by now, where the fuck is it?'

'Patience, Yashi. It will come.'

Below in the cobbled street at the bottom of the hill Alicia heard a sound that alarmed her slightly. From up here, she could not only see everything, but she could hear all the sounds too, mingling together into a hubbub of noise. So why would one scream stand out above the rest? Because she had heard it before, that's why. Turning her attention away from the boat and its containers, Alicia focussed her eyes on a small doorway where the screaming was coming from until suddenly it ceased. Two men exited the door, locking it behind them and she watched them casually walking down the street and along the harbour. Something seemed wrong about them. The larger of the two looked menacing enough, a bald patch on his head gleaming under the street lamps and his face full of scars. But it was the other man that concerned her more, the smooth one in a dark suit. Somehow, he just didn't fit in. Maybe she was just being over cautious.

Then something else struck her. That scream? All of a sudden she knew it now. She had heard it recently, back in the hotel. The pasty little Englishman who seemed permanently confused. Yashi had thought he may be a danger to them, but she was convinced he was harmless enough. But what was he doing down here at the harbour? Alicia dialled another number on her mobile phone and a deep gruff voice answered after two rings.

'You got it?'

'No, not yet. They're still unloading.'

'So why the fuck are you ringing me?'

'Max?' said the Albanian woman, 'I think we have company!' The line went quiet for a minute, before Max answered.

'What sort?'

'Heavy duty. I think I have seen one of them before.' Again the line went quiet for a second, just the sound of heavy breathing, before her instructions came back.

'Keep an eye on them, but don't let them see you. You got that?'

'Trust me, Max, I am a professional.'

'Well don't fuck it up.'

'Oh, and Max?'

'What now?'

'You don't know anything about a little Englishman, do you?'

'What? What the fuck are you on about?'

'Goes by the name of Hard..?'

'Hard?'

'Yes. He turned up at our hotel,'

'So?'

'And he mentioned your name.' Alicia held the phone away from her ear as the man coughed before settling back into heavy breathing again. Half a minute passed before he spoke again.

'Where is he now?' he said calmly.

'I think he might be nearby.'

'Well, if he gives you any trouble, kill him!'

9

Like all good gangsters, Max Hornsby had started early. Born in a fifties housing development in the rougher end of Hockley Heath, his mother had kept a job at what was then the Lucas factory, making parts for cars. As a child, the boy had lived with her in a meagre high-rise flat, with no father around to keep him on the straight and narrow. At first he had been told that his father had died in a road accident, but he later learned that he was in prison, a lifer. When he was nine, his mother had a drugged-up boyfriend who, when she was out at work had tried to persuade the boy to do sexual favours for him. This went on for a few weeks until one day, out of sheer fear, Max stabbed him in the crutch with a bread knife and after that things changed. After a quite convincing pack of lies from the man, his mother and the police took his side and Max was branded as a hooligan and taken into care. In the mid 1970's, care homes were very often run under dubious control and in more cases than not, exposed children to even more sexual abuse. By the time Max Hornsby was 12, he had run away so many times that the authorities had given up looking for him, and he settled into a gang in Birmingham's underworld, living in a deserted big house near Handsworth. To prove his standing amongst the bad men with whom he now associated, two months after he had run away from the home for the last time, Max set fire to it during the night, causing the death of its proprietor and one other person. Despite some pretty strong evidence and a thorough search for the boy, Max was never found or arrested for the crime.

Then, his big break came during the race-riots of the late 70's. While everyone was on the streets battling with the police, Max had set himself up with a small warehouse under a deserted railway arch, and looted as many shops as he could, amassing quite a considerable stash of electrical and other goods. He then found outlets for his booty using small ads in the newspapers and soon there was a considerable queue at his sordid door, as he bought and sold just about anything that was of dodgy origins. As the racial uprising was squashed by heavy handed policing towards the end of the decade, Max's operation came under scrutiny from the local police and the only way he could keep his operation going was through some pretty hefty bribery. Within a few years, he had gained some good contacts amongst the force, especially through gifts of TV's and other goods to the families of some quite high ranking officers, which allowed his business to grow. Under the protection of some fairly heavyweight members of the Serious Crime Squad, Max Hornsby branched out into other areas of crime, surrounding himself with a few of the hardest criminals in the area. Not that he couldn't handle himself; that had been proven a few times, especially during one incident when about 20 people witnessed him brutally killing one of his rivals with a brick-hammer and then pushing him in the canal. He did get arrested for that one, but after a short time in the interrogation room, it was decided there was not enough evidence to press charges, as many of the witnesses had been too scared to speak up.

By the time Max Hornsby was 21, he was one of the most feared gangsters in Birmingham. By the time he was 25, he was also one of the most wealthy. Now his business enterprises, some of which were even legitimate, extended into property development, internet pornography and credit card fraud. Being a man with some scruples, the one thing that Max refused to touch was drugs. Not only did he never get into dealing in drugs, he was very outspoken against their use, especially when they were being pushed to children. As a result of this firm set of principles, Max had managed to maintain a relationship with the police, exchanging occasional information about the drugs supply chain in Birmingham with a couple of officers whom he knew rather too well, for a blind eye to be turned on some of his other enterprises.

More recently, he had taken on a younger lad who at first had seemed quite bright and Max was prepared to offer him a rather good position amidst his latest enterprise. The fact that the man was gay was of no concern to him; indeed some of his gay employees were extremely trusty servants. Max had visions of grooming this young chap to take over one of his property divisions. That was, until he found out that not only was the man a drugs user but he had also been involved in supplying drugs to a local school. Although this had infuriated Max, he stayed calm, checked out some of the man's contacts, and then set him up for a fall.

Believing that he was now employed by one of the most powerful men in middle England, and furthermore was about to do a hefty drugs deal with him, what Jason Tully had not expected, was that the fall would be from a 6 story building, without a parachute. Before pushing him to his death, Max Hornsby had taken his mobile phone and persuaded Jason to reveal who his drugs contact was and, in terrified panic, the man had said it was the last number he had dialled. Looking down at Jason's untidy body lying in the car-park 20 metres below, Max had dialled that number and threatened the person that answered, despite the pathetic man protesting his innocence. Since that time he had tried the number a few more times but the phone had remained switched off. Although preoccupied with a major business deal of his own that was just going through, Max knew only too well that eventually the contact would switch it on again and he would be able to locate him and, at the flick of his fingers, have him terminated.

Basically, Trevor Richard Yashati Hard was a marked man.

*

French television wasn't something that particularly interested Ludovic Broule, he was more of a book man. Mainly he read drama stories and biographies, but sometimes he would read a few detective stories and laugh at how ridiculous they were compared to ordinary police work. Complicated plots about cops and robbers, with intrigue and suspense, were all very well in a glamorised story, but in the experience of all his years in policing nothing like that ever really happened. Until tonight that is.

So far he had changed his opinion of what was going on at least 3 times and, eventually, he had taken to writing it down. In fact he was enjoying it so much he had to work hard to persuade himself not to get involved. Well, maybe he could, just a little bit.

Checking that nobody was watching, Broule heaved his shoulder against the door for the third time, feeling the lock giving way. Inside all was silent as he pushed the door open inwards and flicked on the light. A smile spread across his face, the inhabitant was still alive but just snoring loudly. That was good. His conscience wouldn't have let him leave a murder unreported. On the table beside the sleeping Englishman were a police badge and a mobile phone. Broule made a note of the name and number on the badge, switched off the light and left again, leaving the door unlocked.

*

Meanwhile, Baxter had made his way down a different street and was now checking out the harbour. In his suspicious mind, any one of these containers could be full of illegal substances and he was quite surprised there weren't sniffer dogs on site, seeking out millions of pounds worth. After slipping on a yellow hard-hat and fluorescent jacket that he had found in an empty hut by the entrance to the lorry park, Baxter sidled amongst the waiting lorries, keeping an eye out for Hard, or anyone else that may be suspicious. It wasn't an easy task and a few times he narrowly missed being run over by the shunter wagons that ferried containers back and forth at great speed.

On the way down the street he had found a public phone and tried to call the station back in England. However, the desk sergeant had refused to accept a collect call from a French number, assuming that it may have been a crank call. Not everyone in the department knew that Baxter was working on an under-cover assignment overseas, and generally he liked to keep it that way. Recently the police had been besieged by hoax calls about all sorts of things, a craze that seemed to be spreading through the school kids as the latest way to get their kicks. It was no real surprise that the wily old sergeant wasn't falling for someone pretending to be one of their officers calling from a French seaside town at 11pm. He would have tried to call Rich's mobile phone but he couldn't recall the number. No, for now anyway, he was on his own. Working alone posed no real problem for Baxter Collins. He was a professional and the fact that he had no money, phone, ID or car keys made this operation even more of a challenge. This was the sort of stuff they had been taught on the advanced training camps that he had volunteered for, when they had been pushed through rigorous routines designed for SAS soldiers. One way or other he would pull in Hard and his cronies, however much the odds were stacked against him. One thing he did have was his stealth and powers of detection. Also, he had some cable-ties down the inside of his jacket and a knife in his boot which his attacker had not managed to find. Yes, in Baxter Collins' mind, he was still one step ahead of the game.

Up ahead in the distance, one of the drivers stepped down from his cab and lit a cigarette, looking around impatiently as Baxter slunk back into the shadows out of view. The man was waiting for a pick-up; that was fairly obvious. But then, most of the drivers here were waiting to pick up something, as their empty trailers were loaded with a heavy cargo container, one by one, which was clamped into place before they headed off to who knows where. Unlike most lorries, which bore the name of the owner and often a description of its contents emblazoned on the side in huge letters, cargo containers only had a number printed on them, which was cross referenced through an administration process. To Baxter, every single one was suspicious. But then again, if they were carrying drugs, they wouldn't have that written on the side would they? They would hardly bear the words:

COLUMBIAN HEROIN INC or AFGHANISTAN DRUGS CARRIERS LTD.

Baxter only hoped he wasn't too late to catch Hard doing his deal.

*

As Try awoke for the second time his mind was even more confused than before. During the last 15 minutes he had had the most incredible dream, where he had been on the beach with a beautiful woman called Alicia. In it, she had carried him over her shoulder and thrown him down on the hard sand, ready to make love to him. Her strong hands had caressed his genitals while she asked him questions as the heat rose up around him. But, somehow, she had morphed into a hideous looking giant of a man with hands like snow-shovels inflicting pain that made him scream. Another man in a dark suit was asking the questions now, so many difficult questions it felt like he was a lone contestant on a TV quiz programme for Mensa. And the pain was too much.

Instinctively, Try reached down and checked that he still had two testicles. Thankfully he did, but they were very sore. He closed his eyes and tried to imagine Alicia caressing them again, calling out her name softly into the darkness.

'Alicia, my love. Alicia..'

That was it! At that moment, he had a revelation. Opening his eyes wide, he stood unsteadily to his feet, a smile spreading across his face.

'Alicia, my love,' he said again, whispering now as he fell to one knee. 'Alicia, my love. Will you marry me?'

Whatever had happened during the last few hours, wherever he was now, none of that mattered anymore. He just had to find this girl and ask her to marry him.

As if this had injected Try with a new burst of energy, he jumped to his feet, tripped over a chair and then a table before he eventually found a light switch. Everything seemed like a haze to him now, as he squinted around the small sparsely furnished apartment trying to remember how he got here. Nothing was familiar, despite his best efforts at recollection. Although he knew he must hurry, Try went to the sink, and poured himself a glass of water, sitting back down at the table again.

Right, let's start with the basics. Where am I?

After a couple of bangs on the head, Try's conscience had become a bit more fragmented, sorting many of his thinking cells into individual compartments, not unlike the post office.

'*A sparsely furnished apartment with pink walls and a painting on the wall. Are those sunflowers?*' said the part that did the logical analysis.

'Does it matter what sort of flowers they are?' questioned another bit.

'Well. I don't recognise any of it. Does anyone else?' None of the other compartments did, although one did think that the sofa smelled faintly of cheese.

OK, we had better try an easier one. Who am I?

'Hmm. My Lord doth compose a fine question,' said a philosophical part.

'I can remember being in the Army,' said another, 'and climbing the assault course while Sergeant Bloody Whatshisnane shouted at us.'

'Really? Yes, I do vaguely. But I don't think it was recent,' said frontal logic.

Try closed his eyes. No he not only didn't know where he was, he had no idea who he was either.

All he knew was that he was in love with a beautiful woman and that it was imperative that he asked her to marry him as soon as possible. On the table in front of him was a leather wallet which, again, he didn't recognise.

'That's a clue, that is,' suggested one of his cells.

He picked it up, turning it over in his hand inquisitively before flipping it open. Inside was a credit card bearing the name: Baxter J Collins.

'There you are, told ya!'

'Hang on. Are you sure? Can't say I recognise the name,' questioned Logic.

Opening the wallet further, there were a couple more credit cards both bearing the same name, and a fist full of notes in foreign money. Try stared at them, totally mystified.

'Euros! Why would we carry euros?' And yet somehow, the notes did seem familiar, somewhere in the recesses of his brain that didn't speak for itself. Raising his head, he looked around the room again. In the corner was a small TV and he switched it on. A cop in blue uniform was speaking to a villain in a foreign language, before pulling a gun and shooting him in the stomach, scarlet coloured blood blasting out in all directions. It made Try feel queasy and he turned it off quickly. Then he noticed another wallet on the table, a smaller thin one with a crown embossed on the front. Guessing this was the key to this mystery, Try flipped it open, read the inscription inside and let out a short scream.

Slumping back down into the chair, he read it again and again.

BAXTER J COLLINS – HER MAJESTY'S POLICE FORCE – DRUG ENFORCEMENT.

As his compartments were desperately trying to process the new information that he was actually a Drug

Enforcement Officer, a mobile phone rang on the chair next to him, causing him to nearly jump out of his skin. He picked it up and held it to his ear.

'Baxter?' said the caller in not much more of a whisper. Try dropped the phone like it was made of molten iron and it landed noisily on the tiles beneath him.

'Bax?' continued the call. 'Bax, it's me, Rich. Reg called me to say he had a hoax call from someone pretending to be you. From overseas. I put two and two together and guessed it must be you phoning in. I am at home with the family now, but thought I should just check it out. How's things there in France? Are you OK?'

Try stared at the object as if it was going to attack him at any moment. Eventually he picked it up again.

'Err. Hello?'

'Bax? Are you alright?'

'Err. Yes. I am fine. I was just having a sleep. But I must go now. Bye-bye.' He ended the call and placed the phone back on the table, staring at it again for a few minutes, trying to work out what the caller had said.

'France?' shouted an internal voice. Before the other voices could question it further, Try remembered that he had a beautiful girl and he was intending to marry her. France and the police force could wait. Standing to his feet again, he went over to the sink, splashed some cold water on his face, picked up the wallet and phone and headed out in the La Rochelle night in search of his beloved - as Baxter Collins.

*

From her viewpoint on the balcony, a couple of things disturbed Alicia. One was that shifty looking man hanging around in the lorry park who looked and acted very much like a policeman. He could cause trouble if he got too close. Instinctively she knew she had better keep an eye on him.

The other and more immediate problem was hearing her name repeatedly being shouted out in the street below as it echoed around the narrow streets. Not just her name either.

'Alicia, I love you!'

She watched the Englishman stumble out into the promenade along the harbour, keeping her head down in case he glanced up. 'Alicia! Where are youuuu?!'

It was like watching a child playing a game of hide and seek. Only, to her, this night was no time for games. If he got involved with the authorities, he would surely alert them to her little operation.

Alicia had checked out the man's wallet, which she had since chucked in a waste bin. He lived in some ordinary apartment, worked an ordinary job and, from what she could establish, had lived a fairly ordinary life. As far as she could tell, he was just another tourist. Except, through her own stupidity, he was now smitten with her. Alicia had been used to having this affect on men.

Ever since she had been at school in Warsaw, boys and men had fallen for her good looks. Generally, she had used it to her advantage and, as she developed a more ruthless streak, it had got her into places that others couldn't.

Born Marisa Zobrinsky to wealthy parents, Alicia had grown up in a small but fairytale-like castle in the Polish countryside which had once belonged to a Countess. Blessed with angelic good looks and ringlet curls, the young girl had easily managed to get the better of her parents, as well as the endless streams of maids and servants that were put in place to look after her and her younger sister. At the age of eleven, Alicia was sent to an expensive all-girls school in Warsaw where she excelled at sport but, although she was highly intelligent, was bored rigid with academics. On a weekend trip to stay with one of her friends in Latvia, aged 15, she had been introduced to the girl's brother, Niko, who had quite an unhealthy obsession with guns. It was here that she had handled and fired her first AK47 and it was here that the boy had handled her in return. Drawn by his military prowess, Alicia had been quite taken by this sturdy boy, and a relationship had developed via letters back and forth to her boarding school. After seeing him a few times in the winter holidays, 6 months later, when Alicia had sent him a note to say that she was locked in her dormitory as a punishment for repeatedly swearing at the headmistress, the boy had turned up outside the gates in a military land-rover and broken in to rescue her. Together they had run away and hid out in the mountains, falling in with a gang of rebels who were fighting against the establishment in the name of solidarity and freedom. Under the spell of this wannabe terrorist, the girl had cropped her hair and changed her name to Alicia so that she fitted in with the others.

However, Alicia never really shared the stringent beliefs of her childhood sweetheart, who was obsessed with breaking down the whole Eastern block communist regime. Having come from a family of abundant wealth, she would often share her ideas with Niko, that somewhere beneath all the communist rulers, was a stash of money and jewellery that had been confiscated during the revolution and that, under the smokescreen of battle, they could steal some of it and set up home somewhere. Although he too came from a wealthy background, Niko had no wanton for material possessions and eventually their difference of opinions had caused them to row continuously as the girl pushed forward her own plans. Eventually one day she had snapped, stole a jeep and headed to Albania.

Again using her exceptionally good looks and charming smile to her own advantage, Alicia soon worked her way into an underground gang who were part of larger Mafia organisation, smuggling arms out of Eastern Europe into Africa. Quickly she moved up through the ranks of this outfit, by selectively sleeping with the men who had their finger on the power button, until she was one day summoned to a meeting with the big boss himself. At this meeting, he outlined a new operation that they were setting up across Eastern Europe smuggling not arms, but people. Hearing of her high reputation as a negotiator, he promoted her to the main point of contact between them and a tightly knit criminal gang operating out of middle England. For the last two years, this operation had been highly successful, delivering up to 100 illegal immigrants into the UK per month, and for that, Alicia had been paid handsomely. She also had never forgotten her original plans, especially now she had a network of contacts back in Poland.

For most of the time she worked with an Albanian sidekick called Yashi, when the two of them would pretend to be brother and sister. She didn't think Yashi was his real name but it didn't bother her, as long as the two of them shared the same surname on their fake passports. What did bother her was Yashi's attitude towards others. Here was a man who was unhappy to be out of his country and held underlying beliefs that the whole western world was a corrupt hell-hole full of bigoted hypocrites. Some would say he did have a point here, but Alicia wished that he would keep his opinions to himself. In the opposite way that Alicia's technique was to smile and sweet-talk her way out of just about any situation, Yashi's was to shoot his way out. This was the reason that they had now relocated their latest shipments through the Atlantic port of La Rochelle, because Yashi's name and picture had become quite well know amongst the gendarmes in most of the ports on the Mediterranean after incidents firstly in Marseilles and then Antibes earlier in the year.

Down in the street, her little English pursuer was still calling her name as she watched him through her field glasses heading towards the lorry park. It seemed that not only was he declaring his love for her, but that he also wanted to marry her. Marriage? Now there was something that Alicia had always dreamed of; a big white wedding to a handsome and wealthy man with a string of polo ponies and her own Ferrari. Somehow, she didn't consider that Mr Hard was a contender.

'Al-eeeeee-shaaa!' called out the shell-shocked confused Try, 'where arrrrr you?' As he reached the gates to the lorry-park and a man in uniform stopped him and prevented his entry.

'Arrette, Monsieur. Entrance c'est interdit. C'est juste pour les person avec les camion!' Try focussed on the man, not understanding a word he said.

'Have you seen Alicia?' he asked, 'she is beautiful and sexy and lovely and I am going to marry her!'

'Vous avez un passe, Monsieur?' demanded the sentry.

'A pass?' Try thought for a second. 'A pass? Weee! Weeee! A pass...' He fumbled in his pocket and pulled out the small folding wallet, eagerly showing it to the man. 'Police! I am the police. I am......' Try tried to remember who he was before peering down at the wallet himself. 'I am Mr Baxter.' Try's head was starting to spin again and he needed a sit down. 'Je swiii..... Mon-sewer Bax-ter.... Like the tins of soup!'

To his amazement, and to the amazement of quite a variety of onlookers, the sentry pulled his hand up in a smart salute.

'Entrez, Monsieur Collins!'

*

Cargo containers, by definition, are designed to carry all types of material. Generally, they are about 10 metres long, 3 metres wide and made of heavy duty steel to withstand up to a few months at sea. Usually they are sealed and would, if required during extreme circumstances, probably float for a while. That is, unless they were of a special design, say with a few small air-holes in the upper sides and fitted with a false wall to hide a secret compartment. One thing is for sure, whilst they are in transit, they are most definitely locked.

'Overt!' shouted the one Customs officer above the noise of an overhead crane. Alicia watched her supposed brother unlock the container and swing its doors open. Although this had happened a few times before, she still held her breath as the men shone powerful torchlight inside, looked at each other, and nodded. Yashi closed the double doors and followed the Customs man into his little office.

'C'est beaucoup du velo?' said the man, in French.

'I do not understand French,' answered the driver.

'That's a lot of bicycles, Monsieur?' he repeated in English. Yashi just shrugged.

'I'm just a driver.'

The officer carried on checking his computer screen against the numbers on the paperwork in front of him as Yashi stepped back out of the office, nervously glancing up at Alicia on the balcony. 'Come on...,' he muttered under his breath in Albanian. This was always the hardest part, waiting for customs clearance. Overhead, the cranes clanked and rattled, drowning out any possible noise that may have come from inside this particular container. As he waited, someone tapped him on the shoulder and he swung around.

'Yashi?'

Yashi glared at the man, pretending he never seen him before.

'Yashi. It is you, isn't it? I know it's you.'

'Go away!' hissed the Albanian.

'But Yashi…I have to find your sister. I am in love with her.' Try put his hand on Yashi's arm and the man pushed him backwards. Still unbalanced after being drunk and then knocked out, twice, Try fell backwards onto the tarmac.

'Get lost!' he snarled again.

'Tout ca va?' asked the second Customs officer, appearing from behind another container and looking at Try struggling to get up from the ground.

'Yes, it's fine. This man is a bit drunk, that's all.'

'I am looking for my lover!' said Try, regaining his feet.

'Ignore him,' said Yashi. Try stood there swaying for a moment.

'You mustn't ignore me. I am a police officer! And I am looking for someone.' A sudden look of shock rose in Yashi's eyes, just as the second man came out of his office.

'Tu est l'agent?' said the first man, suspiciously.

'What?' replied Try, confused as to why people kept saying incomprehensible things to him.

'It's OK!' said Yashi, hurriedly. 'He is looking for my sister.' He smiled at the two men, collecting the piece of paper the man was proffering to him. 'It's OK. Come on

mate. I know where she is. I'll take you to her now.'
Before Try could argue, Yashi gripped him firmly by the
arm and ushered him back across the lorry-park.

'I love your sister and I want to marry her,'
protested Try, struggling to make his feet move fast
enough to keep up with the taller Albanian.

'Sure you do!'

'I love her because she is beautiful, and I love her
because she is sexy, and I love her because she is Albanian
and …Where are we going?'

'Just come with me, and we will meet up with her
real soon.'

'She doesn't know it yet, but she is in love with me
too, you know. It was love at first sight,' babbled Try,
following the man down between a row of closely parked
lorries. 'We will get married and have children and
everything….'

'Right, that's far enough, bozo!' snarled Yashi.
When Try turned around he was facing the barrel of a
revolver aimed at his forehead. 'You idiot, you nearly
blew my cover.' He indicated to the ground. 'Now on your
knees and say your prayers, fuckwit!'

'You can't shoot me,' screamed Try, 'I am not a
fuckwit, I am a policeman! I am Campbell Baxter Whosit.'

He tried to reach into his pocket to produce the badge as proof but the Albanian cocked his weapon.

'Goodbye, Mister Hard!'

'Help!' screamed Try, as the sound of a gunshot rang out into the night.

10

Nobody really likes darkness. Yes, some more gothic members of the human race say they do, but they don't really. In the same way that Eskimos will tell you they enjoy the cold, and then go and light a fire. Two whole days of darkness can do strange things to a person, especially if most of that time has been spent in an extremely cramped environment, rocking about on the ocean.

But expectation is a wonderful tonic, and Mimosa had built her entire life around it. Compared to some of the hardship she had endured during her life, this trip was just like being on holiday. It was the others that were the problem. And there were quite a few of them.

Mimosa had been born as a Polish peasant and she had maintained that economic level for all her 33 years. The word peasant is considered as a derogatory term by some, but in actual fact it is a quite acceptable social status. Working the land to provide yourself and your family with food is the first and foremost basic skill required by the human race and something that very few in the western world now possess. At the age of 9, her father had died from pneumonia leaving her mother to bring up 3 girls in a wooden house with little or no heating. Mimosa had worked hard, fetching firewood and water from a well some distance away, as well as tending to the one cow and few sheep that provided them with milk and meat. Then, 2 years later, her mother had died too, from a broken heart and a broken leg, which had gone septic with poison. Mimosa was now head of the house, tasked with the responsibility of bringing up herself and her two younger sisters.

As a young girl, her father had told her bedtime stories about animals in the woods that could sing and dance and she had loved those moments so dearly. He had also made her promise that when she was older she would learn to read and be educated; something that had never been afforded to him. When she was eight and her father was poorly, she would sit up with him through the night, reading through a copy of Hello! magazine which he had brought her from the village, its every page worn and faded as she had thumbed over the beautiful dresses and fashion that only the rich and famous could afford. He had told her that one day she could be rich and famous, as his ancestors had been years ago, but she would have to travel far away from here.

'Mimi, there is a world out there that is ours to share,' he used to say, poetically. In his dying breath, he had held her hand and whispered in her ear.

'Promise me. Once you have seen your sisters grow up, you will go far away from here and find yourself a rich young man in the West.' She had promised him with a final squeeze of the hand as he coughed the last of his life from his lungs.

Unfortunately, it wasn't that easy and in place of a rich young man, at the tender age of 16, she had found a desperately poor one. The boy's name was Prego and he had been thrown out of his own family for being useless and unwilling to contribute to their daily hardships with any work. Mimosa had taken pity on him and taken him in, much against the advice of everyone around her. The man had brought very little with him except a bottle of vodka and, on that first night he had wooed her into bed, tipsy from the alcohol, and taken advantage of her naivety. By the time the baby was born, he was long gone, staggering out of the door drunk one evening, never to return.

In their small and humble hovel, the family cycle had begun again, as Mimosa, like her mother before her, struggled on as a peasant, working 18 hours per day to provide for her family. Over the next few years, the baby boy, Boric, grew up and Mimosa tried to help him learn to read. Out of kindness to this poor weary soul, a neighbour who had been to school came round twice per week and Mimosa and her son learned to read together. It was hard going for her, but she tried to spend a little time learning each evening, despite being utterly exhausted. At first she just learned Polish but then the kind man had given her an English dictionary that his father had brought home after being a prisoner of war in England.

Mimosa had dug out that old copy of Hello! Magazine, and translated every word of the English text, bringing the pictures to life now she understood what the famous celebrities were saying.

While she toiled away at home, one by one her two sisters had found men of their own and left home to work in factories, leaving her a slightly easier life with her son. Then, when he was old enough, Mimosa took the young boy along to a school some 5 miles away, walking there and back twice per day and sometimes carrying the child.

By the age of twelve, it was Boric who was teaching his mother things, repeating to her what he learned at school about History, Geography and Mathematics. All this time, Mimosa had remembered what her father had told her, about 'a whole world out there, for us to share!' The boy was bright and understood what she was telling him, but he also had a love for his country which was changing rapidly and, despite her trying and trying to persuade him, he had no intention of leaving. When he left school at 14, the boy took a job on another larger farm and started bringing in a wage. Although their lifestyle improved with the extra income, Mimosa still harboured the wanderlust and the promise that she had made her father to get out of this place.

Saving no more than a few shillings per week, over a two year period she had amassed enough savings to prepare for a one way trip to the promised land: England. With Boric's help, she had contacted an agency run by some local ruffians who had shown her ragged brochures depicting Windsor castle and the M25 motorway around London. They had promised her a secure passage, a steady job and luxurious accommodation in London, all for the worthy sum of £500. Although Boric was none too sure about the credentials of this local gang of smugglers, his mother had been so determined to get away from this place that he gave her the rest of the money and his blessing. On a dusty June afternoon, Mimosa jumped on to the back of a rickety station-wagon, and waved her last goodbyes to her son as she set out on an adventure that she had dreamed of all her life.

Within the next twenty four hours, this poor exhausted and emaciated young woman had been bundled in with a dozen others into the back of an ex-army truck that bumped its way across the arid plains of Ukraine and Romania towards the Albanian border. Mimosa was only one of two women, the rest being young men, many with dubious backgrounds and scruples. At least 3 times she had to fight off the advances of one randy ex-soldier who insisted on sitting next to her and running his hand over her thigh. Eventually she had slapped him and the others had laughed, but the man had turned angry and hit her back, swearing to get revenge after being humiliated. An hour before they reached the border, the wagon pulled to a halt outside a deserted army billet where they were to spend the night under armed guard. After a meagre ration of Hungarian stew, Mimosa teamed up with the other woman, who was at least twice her age and they shared a bed, hoping to protect each other from the men around them. As expected, during the night the man did pay her a visit, dragging her from the bed and demanding sex, but the old woman had been used to this sort of behaviour from her now deceased husband and fought the man off with a stick, thrusting it hard into his private parts until he screamed with pain, alerting one of the guards. After the guard had dragged him away and given him a severe beating, the old woman admitted that she had eventually murdered her own husband in similar manner, except she had used a sword, which was the reason she was now looking for asylum and a new life. Mimosa felt a bit more comforted after that.

The next day, like a flock of sheep, they were loaded up a ramp into a livestock transporter, where they were to lie quietly on the top deck while real sheep and a few goats took up the lower one. The smell had been quite unbearable and without anything more than the clothes she stood up in – or in this case lay down in - plus a small carrier bag with a few basic possessions, the journey had been agony as the lorry bumped along sandy tracks towards the coast.

As they were unloaded into a holding pen next to the other livestock, Mimosa caught her very first sight of the sea, and thought its gleaming surface and distance horizon were enchanting. Within a few hours, and for a whole day afterwards, her opinion of the ocean dramatically changed.

*

It wasn't just by pure chance that Baxter had spotted Hard walking across the car-park with another man, he had been eyeing him up for a few minutes beforehand and had seen the lorry driver push him to the ground. This seemed an unlikely performance for two drugs contacts but, nevertheless, Baxter had now got him in his sights. It wasn't until he had rounded the back of the parked lorry that he realised that it was in fact someone else who had Hard in his sights, as he dived on the gunman just in time, deflecting his aim so that the bullet thudded into a lorry tyre. Grabbing the gun from the man's hand, Baxter gubbed the attacker over the head so that he fell down to the ground beside Hard, and then held the two of them at gunpoint whilst he gathered his breath and his thoughts. Was this a drugs deal gone wrong? It must be.

'You can't shoot me! I am Baxter's Soup!' screamed Try again, still with his eyes closed.

'What?' replied the real policeman. Try opened his eyes for a second, trying to focus.

'Stop. I am the police!' he screamed. 'I will have you arrested for...for...taking my woman away!'

Baxter eyed him with suspicion. What on earth was the man burbling on about now?

'You. On your feet,' he said to Yashi, waving the gun. 'Tell me what's going on, and I don't want bullshit.' Yashi stood up but said nothing.

'I am in love with his sister…,' continued Hard. 'She will marry me, or else I will arrest her. And him. And you…I am…,' Try put his hand in his pocket again and pulled out the wallet. 'I am Baxter Collins, Her Majesty's Wossit.'

'Give me that, you prat!' shouted Collins above the noise of a ship's foghorn.

'No!' Try put it back in his pocket. 'You can't shoot me. I am Baxter Collins!'

'Don't tempt me!' replied Baxter. Reaching into his own pocket, he pulled out a plastic cable-tie and, using one hand, skilfully pulled it around Yashi's wrist as the man scowled at him. At the same time, he was thinking fast. Hard had managed to get his badge and was now pretending to be a police officer. Well that was an offence right there, but he wanted more from this jaunt. He needed bigger offences than that. This other man was about to kill him in cold blood. Maybe he was from a rival gang? It was possible there would be more than one gang working from this den of iniquity? The foreign looking man was refusing to talk but, as Baxter looked at him, he noticed, just for a fraction of a second, the man glance over his shoulder. That short moment in time was not quite long enough for Baxter to swing around before an iron bar caught him on the side of the head and he slumped to the ground.

'What took you?' said Yashi, sarcastically.

'ALICIA! My darling, where have you been!?' screamed out Try, lurching towards her and stumbling over Baxter's body. With most of his senses still tangled by the alcohol and couple of bangs on the head, he lost his balance and ended up on top of Baxter who was unconscious. Try scrambled to his feet, clawing at the tarmac with his open hands and inadvertently grabbing the pistol. Before he had chance to realise what he was doing, Try squeezed the trigger, loosing off another shot which this time bounced off the metalwork of the trailer he was half lying under, and ricocheted directly into Yashi's left leg.

In the ensuing seconds it was difficult to establish who was screaming the loudest as both Try and Yashi competed for the honour, the former out of fear of firing a loaded weapon and the latter hopping around on one leg. Alicia calmly stepped between them, picking up the gun and holding it in both hands.

'Idiots, all of you,' she snapped angrily. 'Can't you do anything without shooting at people?' The comment was aimed at Yashi, who ignored her as he rolled up the trouser leg of his overalls, checking the wound. It wasn't too serious, just a darkened bruise where the bullet had rattled onto his rigger boot.

'And as for you, Little Englishman, what am I going to do with you?'

'Marry me?' offered Try weakly, finding himself staring into the barrel of the same gun for a third time, each one from a different attacker.

'Yashi. Go and hook up the trailer. We won't have much time before someone finds us, especially if they heard that shot,' she commanded. 'I'll deal with these two.' The man grunted and hobbled on his way as Try managed to get to his feet.

'Alicia, I love you,' he continued, seemingly oblivious to the gun pointing at him and what had gone on around him.

'Shut up, you moron.' Try's eyes focused on her features, filling with water around the edges. 'I should shoot you here and now.'

'You can't do that...,' he was becoming hysterical again. 'You can't do that. I am a policeman!'

'No you're not, you idiot.'

'I am, look...?' Alicia peered at the badge and then at the face-picture of a man with blonde spiked hair.

'Nice try.'

'Thank you.'

'What?'

'Thank you for calling me nice.'

'What?'

'You said nice Try. That's my name.'

'Well, it certainly isn't this guy, is it?' She pointed to the picture, and sighed. 'Does that look like you?' Try looked down at it blankly, and then down at the man lying on the floor. Eventually, the penny dropped. First he shook his head silently, and then nodded his eyes down to the body on the floor.

'Exactly!' For a second Alicia gave a light smile.

'So?'

'What?'

'So? Will you marry me?' Alicia shook her head.

'No, Mister Hard. I will not marry you. I am sorry. Without appearing too rude, I do not think you would make a good husband for me!'

'But...but!' Try stared helplessly at the beautiful woman pointing a loaded gun at him and his heart sank. Uncontrollably, a tear dropped from his cheek.

'Come on you guys, help him out,' cried out his Logical brain compartment, 'I am no good at this sort of thing!'

'Let me have a go,' said one of the emotional sectors.

'But….I can change!' muttered Try, his bottom lip wobbling uncontrollably.

Despite Alicia's mercenary up-bringing and the hardened exterior that she had developed during her eventful life of crime, somewhere inside her this struck a chord and she felt a pang of compassion bubbling away. Get a grip! she told herself. Kill him now and get on with your job. Alicia's finger tightened on the trigger as she looked into the pathetic man's eyes. Somewhere in his whining and his declaration of love for her, this little man had weakened her heart.

'Oh. Come on,' she sighed eventually, grabbing him by the arm. 'But no more talk of love, OK? You don't love me. I won't marry you. But, for your nerve, I won't kill you.' She frogmarched the man out into the open, just in time to see a white lorry coming into view with a yellow container on the trailer behind it. 'I just hope you like bicycles.'

Try blinked in the headlights like a particularly dazed rabbit on a very busy highway.

'*Result!!*' yelled out Emotion, metaphorically raising his hand. '*High five!*'

*

'Did that sound like gunshots to you?'

'I never heard nuffin?'

'Well, I did. I reckon it was coming from that lorry park. Come on Serge, keep up.' K was already running towards the park when a lorry came around the corner, an overhead street-lamp lighting the driver's face up in orange. Pulling his partner back from view, he dropped his voice down to a whisper.

'That's him. That's them,' he hissed. Taking a pen and paper from his suit pocket, K scribbled down the registration number of the lorry and then the identification number on the side of the container.

'You go back to the town, fetch the car and meet me here, pronto.'

'Why me?' complained Serge, 'can't I stay and rough 'im up a bit?'

'Just get going!'

While he was gone K sneaked a little closer and then pulled a camera from his pocket. He could see the lorry pulling to a stop, as two figures appeared in the headlights in front of it. K checked the micro-camera had the flash switched off, and then fired off a few shots.

'Just doing my job,' he mumbled to himself, 'you never know when those will come in handy.' As he watched, the back doors of the lorry were opened and a familiar man was ushered inside, pushed down amongst the boxes and then the doors slammed again. It was the woman they had followed earlier, her chiselled features silhouetted in the dim light as she looked his way. 'That's it, my girl, smile for the birdie!' he whispered to himself. Then, with a rev of the engine, the lorry pulled away, circling around in an arc and following the sign for exit. K let it go.

*

You don't spend time as a Parisian detective, not to recognise the sound of gunshots above all other noises. Officer Broule had been keeping an eye on the two thugs, who in turn had been watching the lorry car-park by the harbour. Unlike the other two, Broule had also noticed the pretty girl sitting on an upstairs balcony. She was the one that intrigued him most and, from his experience of women, she looked far and away the most dangerous. He had seen her leave the upstairs room, turning off the light as she went, and watched her scurry across to the park round about the same time the first shot was fired. Broule noted the exact time in his notebook. Wow what a story. And it wasn't over yet as, shortly afterwards, the second shot was fired. In the distance, he made out a man hobbling to a lorry, then the lorry returning, the container opened, something thrown in, and it drive off.

Next he witnessed a car drive up, collect a man in a dark suit, and follow the lorry. This was like an episode of the keystone cops. When the two vehicles had gone out of sight, Broule wandered casually over to the lorry park, flashed his badge to the sentry guard and had a look round between a few of the lorry trailers. It didn't take him long to find what he was looking for. He just followed the trail of blood.

*

'What you mean, one extra passenger?' growled Max into the receiver. 'I don't take passengers.'

'A prisoner, then?'

'Nor fucking prisoners! Get rid of the prick!'

'No can do. This one goes with the load. You deal with him your end.' Alicia knew she was playing with fire. It didn't do to cross Max Hornsby, she was aware of that. It wasn't good for business to upset the man. She knew her bosses wouldn't be happy about her sending the Englishman back with the cargo, either, and they still had another ferry to cross yet. But he had seen her face, so she couldn't let him go; and anyway, he was so love-struck, he would probably come looking for her if she did. No. If she could get him back on to British soil, she was convinced he might forget about her and go back to his ordinary life in accounts or whatever mundane career he followed.

'Does he know what's going on?'

'No. He's in the back with the boxes. I am pretty sure he'll stay quiet.'

'Pretty sure? Now you listen here, you dumb Polack, I don't want nobody screwing up this operation. So you pull that rig over and put a bullet in the fucker. Comprend?' The line went dead. Alicia realised maybe she had taken a step too far. Perhaps she would have to do what Max suggested, and deal with the extra passenger after all.

In the back of the container, the extra passenger was starting to come back to his senses, although confusion still ruled with an overwhelming majority. In the darkness, he deduced that he was lying amongst a pile of cardboard. To start with, this made him wonder if he had become homeless? Maybe he had been evicted from his apartment, and was now living rough in a doorway in Corporation Street in Birmingham? His brain worked on the problem for a while, recalling his recent utility bills for gas and electric that may have been left unpaid and that might have caused this eviction order. Then another part of his brain - for Try's brain did indeed have many, many compartments; imagine it like a room full of half-empty left-luggage lockers – it detected that the ground was moving underneath him. This was confirmed when they came to a sudden halt and one rather large cardboard box landed on top of him, smothering him completely. Scrabbling with his hands, he tore the cardboard away to reveal part of its contents which felt remarkably like a bicycle wheel. Again his brain struggled for traction. Why would he be in a moving shed full of bicycles? This conundrum remained unsolved for a considerable time, while the whole cranium server shut down into a confused and exhausted sleep. During that sleep, two or three of the sub-conscious compartments worked together trying to organise some of the facts into multiples of three, while the more creative sector flooded the area with dreams so absurd that the when he did awake, the current real situation would seem comparably normal as a result. As with much of Try's life, simplicity was nowhere to be seen.

Back in the front passenger seat, Alicia considered her options with significantly more logic as the lorry rumbled on through the night towards the port of Calais. With this delivery, she would make enough money to get out of this sordid business and maybe lay low for a while. It was something she had been working on for quite some time and she had to see it through on her terms.

In another compartment of the same lorry – lorries do have numerous compartments, although not as many as Try's brain, and theirs are considerably larger and fuller – snoring could be heard in a variety of pitches. Mimosa did her best to block out the noise with her head-scarf as all the other occupants slept heavily now the motion was that of a smooth motorway instead of the ocean at full swell. It wouldn't be long now, she could feel it. Two days, they had told her, and that was surely nearing its end;

two whole days of near darkness breathing in rancid recycled air. To keep herself occupied, she reviewed the pictures in her mind of castles in the countryside and acres and acres of fields and crops. The others were destined for the big city and a land of opportunity but Mimosa was a country girl, born and bred. For her, the dream was to live in a country where she could feed comfortably off the land; where her and her Prince-charming would have herds of cows and flocks of sheep, grazing exclusively on their own farm. She thought back to the lonely life she had endured, and to Boric and his wanting to make things better.

*

'There they are! Pull in behind them at a safe distance.'

'You sure that's the right one? All these lorries look the same.'

'Just do it, Serge. I'll speak to HQ and see how they want to play it.'

*

Blue lights flashed around the harbour, lighting up the still waters as a crowd of dock workers watched the ambulance men at work, lifting a body on to a stretcher and loading it up through the dimly lit back doors.

Broule had decided that he could no longer stand back and observe this situation that was maybe getting a bit out of hand. Once the ambulance had loaded up the victim, he briefed the local authorities on what he knew, giving them specific details from his notebook.

'When he comes round, hold him in custody and grill him! He's in on this. Whatever this is!' he suggested to the police sergeant. With that he made his way back home, pulled on his uniform, jumped on his motorbike and set off back up the motorway towards Paris. Within an hour he had caught up with the lorry, overtaken it, and kept it in his sights from a distance up in front. All the while, he was trying to piece together who was who and, more to the point, what was in that lorry.

For the next 3 hours, all three vehicles unknowingly travelled in convoy towards Paris.

During that 3 hour stretch, Try had slept, dreamed, woken, screamed, thought about things and then slept again. This time, when he woke, he was sure he could hear voices.

'Hellooo! Can you hear me?'

Absentmindedly, Try sorted amongst the boxes but there was nothing there.

'Hello..' he replied. 'Are you a voice in my head?' Then one his compartments suggested that maybe there were things in the boxes that talked. Like, possibly, talking dolls or something? This part of the brain was known to be one of the less intelligent sectors, but, all the same, it managed to persuade the rest of him to have a closer look.

'But there is just bikes!' he shouted out loud, ripping open one box after another.

'Bikes?' replied a voice.

'Yes, bikes!' Now he was having a conversation with himself but in the interests of balance he decided to continue. Maybe this was a part of his brain that knew things. 'Do you know who I am?' he continued, and then listened inwardly for an answer.

'Mister Bikes?'

Try thought about this but the name didn't sound familiar.

'No!' he answered eventually.

'No?'

'I don't think so. It would be a real coincidence if we're in a lorry full of bikes and my name actually was Mr Bikes, wouldn't it?'

The voice went silent for a minute before it answered.

'Hello.... Mr Bikes?'

'I just told you, I am not Mr….wait a minute! That voice isn't mine. It's female…' Try looked around in the darkness, listening for the voice above the noise of the tarmac rushing underneath him. 'Who are you?' he asked, eventually. Silence followed for a short while and Try was beginning to think he had imagined it again.

Different parts of his brain discussed a few theories until eventually one of them said: *'Are you Alicia?'*

Even that one knew it was a long shot and anyway, argued one of the other parts, Alicia threatened to kill you, and she wasn't very nice to you. She definitely said she didn't want to marry you. This time an answer came back.

'My name is Mimosa.'

'Mimosa? Is that Indian?' questioned Try's international compartment. The question went unanswered. Some more theories arrived that required answers.

'Why are you speaking to me in my head? And, if you are not in my head, then where are you?'

'Poland!'

'Poland?' A few of his brain compartments discussed this between themselves.

'*If she was in Poland, then he must be in Poland, otherwise he wouldn't hear her from all that distance away,*' suggested the logic compartment.

'*What was he doing in Poland?*' asked Geographics.

'*Maybe she's lying?*' piped up a spokes-cell for the Sceptical division. '*Maybe she wants us to think she is in Poland?*' Some of the other cells nodded their heads at this.

'*Let's test her?*' said Logic.

'What is the capital of Poland?' It wasn't really a sensible question but it would at least confirm that she was not in his head, as he had no idea of the answer.

'Warsaw!' snapped a tired answer from the darkness.

'*Did she say Walsall?*' asked Geographics. '*That's not right. Walsall is near Birmingham. We went there last year, remember?*'

Memory bank minor remembered.

'*It was ghastly!*' it said.

'*Did you say Walsall?*' asked Try, trying to be heard above all the confusion. There was silence again.

'*See?*' said Sceptical, '*she doesn't know the answer.*'

'Well, if she doesn't know the answer, then maybe the voice is one of us?' reasoned Logic, 'because we don't know the answer either!'

'But if we don't know the answer, then how do we know it's wrong?' This was one of Logic's little brother's, who had just woken up. 'There could be more than one Walsall?'

'More than one Walsall?! Why would you want more than one Walsall?' argued Geographics. 'Surely, when they built Walsall, they would have realised their mistake and not built another one.'

'What if they built the other one first, and then our one afterwards from the same drawings?'

'What? Like a blueprint for shit towns?' agreed Geographics. 'Yeah, I suppose so. I hadn't thought of that. If you were going to build a shit town, then why not map it out and reproduce it elsewhere. That's good thinking.'

'Hang on,' said Sceptical. 'Why would anyone want to build a shit town in the first place?' Some others nodded. 'Why not build from a blueprint of a nice town? Like Florence, or Miami?'

'Oooh no, we don't want Miami in Birmingham. Think of all the crime? Hockley's bad enough. And all those men in white suits and flowery shirts? It would be unbearable. Florence would be alright, I suppose. Or maybe Skegness…'

'SHUT UP!!!' shouted Try, doing his best to organise the troops, 'I can't hear myself think.'

'*Oh yes you can!*' chorused some of the bolder cells.

'SHUT UP!' he said again.

Behind the metal compartment wall, Mimosa was getting more and more confused as well. Somewhere in her dream she had imagined that she would just be able to make happy conversation in English with anybody she met. But now she was not so sure. Here was a man who spoke in such a confusing language that it would be impossible to learn and certainly not in any of the books she had read. As the girl slumped back down to her seat in the corner, the lorry swung hard to right, forcing her sideways against one of the other sleeping immigrants.

The movement threw Try sideways as well, and he grabbed the handlebars of one of the bikes to rescue himself as the lorry drew to an abrupt halt, its air-bakes making a whooshing sound directly under him. Up until now, Try had never got around to considering where they were going, but maybe they had arrived already. Were they in Poland? What was Poland like....No, don't ask, or else the discussion in his head would rage again. Outside he could hear voices and footsteps. The voices were foreign, just as you might expect in Poland; or Walsall for that matter.

'Mr Bikes? You are in danger. They are going to kill you.' It was the woman's voice that, despite his reservations, he had been assured was not inside his own head. It was whispering this time.

With that, the huge latch that held the back-door closed, clunked open and fresh air gushed in to help cool Try's overheated brain.

'Out!' snarled the foreign voice of Yashi. 'Come on, out!' Try fumbled for a second, as various compartments in his brain tried to piece together what was happening. It took a short while for Logic and Geographics to wake up Athletics, who had been sleeping quite some time – 20 or 30 years maybe. Before Try had chance to resist, his hands, arms and feet were responding of their own free will, as he pulled the bicycle from the remainder of its cardboard box, grabbed at its handlebars and swung a leg across its crossbar. Fortunately for him, it did have a seat. With all the energy that an athlete who has done no physical training for a very long time can muster, at 3 o'clock in the morning, Try cycled out into the night like ET. However, putting appearances on one side, there were a few major differences between ET and Try Hard - a distinct variant in IQ levels for instance. But the main difference was that ET could fly - and Try could not. So rather than fly out into the night, he plummeted the 2 metres that was between him and the ground. Fortunately, Yashi broke his fall and - less fortunately for Yashi – the Albanian man's nose, as the front wheel landed on his head. Miraculously gaining his balance, like a frantic hamster in a large invisible wheel, Try pedalled off into the night as fast as his legs would obey. Behind him, a flurry of gunshots rang out into the night, whistling past his ears as he headed the cycle across the tarmac and dropped down into a dense coppice of trees. Daring not to look round, he was pretty sure he heard another voice that he recognised – that of Alicia shouting after him. Was she trying to save him…..? Or kill him? The consensus of opinion inside his head agreed that it was probably the latter. The consensus also concurred that they may well be in Poland and being tracked though a forest by people who wanted to murder him which - as would most normal people, let alone a deranged paranoid who has been twice recently knocked unconscious and drunk far more alcohol in one sitting than he had in the last 10 years -spurred him on towards oblivion. The fact that he could see absolutely zero through the pitch blackness did nothing to slow his pace. Generally, the situation was, as Sceptical pointed out, an accident waiting to happen. Very shortly, a state of unconsciousness was quickly resumed as his head crashed into an overhead trunk that was hanging low for reasons unknown. The last thought that Logic could proffer was that *in moments like these, it is advisable to wear a cycle helmet!'*

In the distance, a lorry restarted its engine and continued on its journey, as the driver held a bloodied handkerchief to his nose while listening to vehement shouting from his female passenger.

'You bloody idiot!' she screamed in Albanian. 'You let him get away! What if he goes to the police?'

'I am pretty sure I hit him. And, anyway, I don't think the police would believe him. The man's a lunatic. Just calm down! OK?'

'I won't calm down. He has seen my face. The man will remember me!' For a full 10 minutes the argument raged on, with Alicia getting more and more angry. The one time she had needed her partner to do some shooting and he had failed. Still, somewhere in her heart, she had been secretly glad that she hadn't had to witness the cold blooded murder of an innocent bystander. But with him at large, things may get a bit more tricky in future. Alicia didn't think he would go to the police and if he did, Yashi was right, he didn't have any real evidence.

In the car behind them, Serge was getting angry too.

'But they stopped! We could 'ave jumped 'em!' moaned the big oaf of a man, scratching at his stubbly chin.

'We watch and we follow. OK? That's our orders.' K rolled his eyes. Serge really was a loose-cannon. Yes the lorry had just pulled over into a lay-by for a minute or two. Maybe the driver had needed a piss and didn't want to risk using a service station. K had made the decision not to follow them too closely and suggested they stayed on the highway, slowing down to steady pace until it caught them up again. He knew it was risky, but was fairly certain that the lorry couldn't unload its cargo in that small area. From his professional experience, he also knew that if they had followed it in, they would have undoubtedly been spotted. Eventually they had pulled over onto the hard shoulder, and thankfully, after no more than a few minutes, the lorry appeared on the highway again, still heading north. This time they pulled away before it reached them, keeping ahead of it for a while so that its driver wouldn't notice them tailing it. Their chance would come.

Officer Broule had taken a slightly different approach. When he spotted the big lorry in his rear view mirror indicating that it was leaving at the last exit, he accelerated up to 150 kph. Broule knew this road like the lines on his own face. Within half a minute he had reached another exit, this one marked with a no-entry sign which was used for service vehicles only. In this instance, a police motorbike counted as a service vehicle as he swung the powerful machine around on the gravel and along a dirt road that led back down to the lay-by, dropping his headlights. As he neared he could make out a silhouette of the lorry through a hazy orange light coming from a row of toilets, and the sound of voices. Switching off the motorbike's engine he pulled to a halt, put the machine up on its stand and watched as the back doors were opened. Up until now, Broule had thought he was following a bunch of villains, maybe running some stolen goods, but now his opinion changed again as something flew out of the lorry, at 2 metres high and then disappeared into the dense thicket. Scratching his head, at first he wondered if maybe it was some sort of alien escaping to find its mother craft. But it wasn't until the sound of half a dozen gunshots rang out, that he made his final assessment. These people were importing wild animals and releasing them out into the wilds of France. The gunshots would have been to scare the beast away so that it didn't attack its handler. He was even more convinced, when he heard the sound of high pitched screaming heading away into the thick forest, that something between a hyena and a wild bear was now on the loose. Within minutes, the lorry continued on its journey and Broule was torn between following it or seeking out the animal. As a hunting man he decided on the latter, on the understanding that he could catch up with the lorry later and, anyway, he could always radio ahead if his suspicions were confirmed. Checking his pistol was loaded he climbed back on to his motorbike, started the engine as quietly as he could and followed the trail of the beast, gun at the ready. Hunting was usually only a winter sport for Broule, and one that he thoroughly enjoyed. Since the end of his days of chasing down villains in the city streets this was the only time he ever got to fire a weapon and, ever since he was a boy, Ludovic was a pretty good shot. When the forest got too thick, he pursued the beast on foot.

Then, when he stopped and listened, the screaming sound had ceased now but he heard another noise, a clicking sound. Maybe it was lying in wait for him? Broule held his gun out in front with both hands, trying to focus in the darkness. Still unable to see through the total blackout, he pulled out a torch, aimed it into the bush, held his breath and switched it on. Instantly the beam bathed the area in yellow light, highlighting something glinting beneath a low tree. It was going round slowly.

'Un Velo?' he whispered to himself, confused. It wasn't until he got a bit nearer that he saw the figure of a man, lying in the darkness. Broule rolled him over with one foot, shining the light on it face.

'Vous?' he snapped, raising his head to the night sky. 'Ooh-la-la!'

Briefly, the bright light caused Try to open one eye, but what that eye saw made his senses close it very fast. A soldier standing over him with a pistol, talking in a foreign, probably Polish, tended to make that happen. After yet another bang on the head, some of the compartments of his brain refused to wake up this time, throwing in the proverbial towel and shutting down. Eyesight reported back to Recognition that they were probably in grave danger, not that it was their job to deal with that. A message was passed to Logic who tended to be better at making decisions on matters such as this. Except that Logic had gone fishing for the weekend, leaving one of his understudies in charge, who was still learning his craft.

'Pretend we are asleep and then jump up and surprise him..,' it suggested, helpfully.

'Surprise him!? He's got a bloody gun, you idiot! Surprise him and he'll fire it! Then what would we do, with bloody great hole in us?' Sceptical had a headache. 'Don't tell me, don't tell me? We call up Medical and tell him to bring a needle and cotton!'

'It was just a suggestion,' mumbled Logic minor. 'You got a better one?'

'Well, as a matter of fact I do,' chipped in Enthusiasm. The other two turned to him in anticipation. 'We all go back to sleep!'

'That's typical, that is! So bloody typical of you! Your solution to everything, that is. Just forget it, eh? Relax? Chill a bit?' Sceptical would have stamped his foot, if he had one. 'Like the time when we fell in the canal? Relax and we'll float, you said. And what happened? We went down like the bloody Titanic!'

'He could have a point though!' replied Logic minor, gaining a little confidence in his new role. 'Maybe if we pretend to be dead, that might work? He wouldn't kill us if he thought we were dead, would he? Who shoots dead people? Come on, gotta be worth a shot?'

Sceptical winced when he heard the word shot, but had to agree, in the absence of most of Try's senses, playing dead was probably their best bet.

'Alright,' he sighed, 'but no jumping up, doing that stupid surprise thing. OK?'

With that, whatever parts of Try's brain that were awake, passed out again. When he woke again, he was sitting in the back of a car.

11

'You sure?' questioned Max, after Alicia had told him that Hard was dead. She knew she was taking a chance but, if need be, she could talk her way out of it later.

'Yes, in the forest. My partner put 3 shots in him a few hours ago.' The man sounded a bit more relaxed at this news.

'Thank fuck for that. What time will you be in Calais?'

'Should be there by..' she checked her watch, '7am, local time.'

'Good. I'll get my people organised.' The line went dead as Alicia thought about this. My people? Max Hornsby had people everywhere, always someone on his payroll helping to grease his path. Instinctively she glanced across to Yashi who was now focussed on driving again. That was the problem with Max. You never quite knew who was on your own side. It had been a long night and she needed some rest.

'You alright driving?' she asked him. The man just nodded, not even glancing over as she slid out of her tight jeans and scrambled up on to the bunk bed behind the seats. 'OK, wake me up 20 minutes before we reach Calais,' she yawned, pulling a blanket up around her and closing her eyes. Alicia found that quite strange. She had a fantastic body that had always made men turn their heads, even if only for a brief moment, yet in all the 6 months she had known him, Yashi had never taken the slightest interest in her at all. Maybe underneath all that butch shoot-em-up exterior, he was gay? It didn't matter. Not long now and she would never have to see him again. All he needed to do was to get them there.

*

Meanwhile, Office Broule was getting nowhere. Having radioed one of his colleagues in the traffic division, the two of them had lifted the unconscious Try out from the deep forest and hauled him in to the back of the squad car. Broule had called this particular officer because he spoke good English and they had driven to a service station. However, he wasn't quite so tactful with his interviewing techniques as Broule, who had had years of practice.

'Give me answers. Now!' shouted the man as Try's eyes opened.

'Arrrgghhh, help, police!' screamed Try. Broule winced, feeling the man's pain.

'We are the police, you imbecile,' he said calmly. 'Here, drink this!' Try accepted a steaming cup of coffee and took a sip, glancing out of the window at a man walking his dog amongst the flowerbeds. Then he looked back at the two officers in uniform.

'But you speak English? Do all Poles speak English?'

'Poles?'

'Yes.' Try blinked innocently as the interviewer was already starting to seethe, assuming 'Pole' was a slang English word for the police, like Pigs or Rossers. He was also in a fairly foul mood after being brought in to help another officer right at the end of his shift. This time he grabbed Try by his shirt collars.

'Give me some answers!' he growled, 'or I will personally drag you down the motorway by one leg behind this car!'

'But I don't know the questions....!'

'Well you can start by telling me who you are?' Try thought about this. He was now being interrogated by Polish police who were going to torture him.

Maybe now was a good time to cooperate, suggested his Logic compartment.

'You don't know who I am?' he said, sitting up and rubbing the bruise on the back of his head.

'No, as a matter of fact we don't.'

'Oh dear!'

'What do you mean – Oh Dear?!' The man tightened his grip but Broule put a steadying hand on his shoulder.

'Marcel, tranquil!' he said quietly, giving him a glare. Marcel continued with his questioning.

'Who are you and what are you up to?'

'That's 2 questions,' answered Try. 'I wish I knew.'

Broule spoke to Marcel in French while Try's brain worked on both questions. It was very difficult as he much preferred things in threes. The third one came soon afterwards and it was at last one that he did know the answer to.

'Bikes,' he replied loudly.

'Bikes?'

'And voices!'

The traffic officer slapped him round the face and Try screamed.

'Bikes and voices! Voices and bikes. That's all I know. They were going to Poland. And Yashi is Albanian….and so is my mother.' He man loosened his grip slightly.

'That's better. Now we are going somewhere.'

'Where?'

'What?'

'Where are we going? You said we are going somewhere?'

'You're going nowhere!' Try blinked his eyes a few times, trying to focus on the dog outside again. This was the second time he had been interrogated in one night.

'I want to go home,' he sniffed.

'To Albania?'

'No. To Walsall. Is it far?'

'Walsall?'

'It's the capital.'

'Of what?'

'Of Poland, dummy. Don't you know the capital of your own country?' This remark solicited another slap from the officer.

'Stop hitting me!'

'Stop hitting you? I haven't even started yet. Now for the last time, tell me who you are? What is your name?'

'I can't remember…'

'Well, start at the beginning.'

'Beginning of what?' The officer raised his hand again. 'Alright…Alright!' Try took a deep breath. 'The last thing I remember was going on holiday to France. To a town called La Rochelle.'

'La Rochelle?' Broule nodded to the officer that this much he already knew.

'But Mrs Meatier attacked me and….'

'Mrs Meatier?'

'Pronounced Met-i-air,' he added wearily. 'She attacked me and I ran away and I don't remember anything after that.'

'Why did this woman attack you?'

'For sex.'

'You wanted to have sex with her?'

'No, I wanted to have sex with Alicia!'

'Alicia?'

'Yes. She is Albanian?'

'Mrs Meatier attacked you because you wanted to have sex with Alicia?'

'Yes. No. No she wanted to have sex with me!'

'Who wanted to have sex with you?'

'Mrs Meatier.' Broule wrote this down. 'And Napoleon.'

'Napoleon?'

'Yes.'

You filthy pervert, thought the officer. A threesome, turning into an orgy.

'Who is Napoleon? Is he Albanian as well?'

'No. Yashi is Albanian. He is the brother.'

'Napoleon's brother?'

'No. Napoleon is a dog!'

Marcel, being a family man brought up with catholic morals, was getting more disgusted by the minute. He had heard about some wild sex parties in some of the more promiscuous towns on the Atlantic coast but this one was outrageous. In his head he did a quick calculation. That was 2 men, 2 women and a dog. Trying hard to hold on to his temper, he took a deep breath and continued.

'Was there anyone else at this party?'

'Party?'

'Well, you probably call it an orgy?'

'Orgy? I have never been to an orgy in my life!' cried out Try, doing his best to keep up with the questions.

Broule was also struggling to keep up with the conversation but he recognised the word dog.

'I shot Napoleon!' he announced to Marcel who nearly swallowed his own tongue.

'When?' he replied in French.

'Well I wasn't at bloody Trafalgar, was I? It was attacking a man in the street, and then he came for me, so I put a bullet in him,' said Broule calmly in his native tongue. 'Now, can we get on with this? Find out what he knows about that lorry and what is inside it?'

For another 5 minutes, Marcel kept the questions coming as Try got more and more confused. The only thing he was reasonably sure of was that it was something to do with the Righteous Brothers, who had hit him on the head, and some bikes. And possibly some samosas, but he wasn't too confident on the last bit.

Eventually the two officers gave up while they still had their own sanity. Inside his own head, just about every compartment was scrambling to be heard until a full blown row was going on between them all. Logic and Sceptic were arguing whether a samosa was Indian or from Bangladesh so loudly that Try was finding himself hard to be heard.

'That's it!' he suddenly shouted. 'Hard. That's me. My name is Trevor Hard!' With that he slumped down in the seat and closed his eyes again.

*

As the lorry swung off the motorway onto the slip road, Alicia opened hers. She hadn't really slept but at least she had rested for a while.

'Yashi, I thought I told you to wake me half an hour before Calais?' The man just grunted and rubbed his tired eyes as Alicia reached for her jeans and pulled them on over her long legs. 'Right, we need to go over the plan one more time!' She slid her athletic body down from the bunk and back into her seat as her mind ran over what she was about to say.

'Is easy. Same as last time!' said her partner.

'No Yashi. It's not the same. This time we do things differently.'

'Differently? What is differently about this time?' Alicia looked across at the tired man, he wasn't going to like this bit. That's why she hadn't told him till now.

'This time, we take the goods all the way!'

'I know this. We take the container all the way to the dock. Then we unhook the trailer. Is easy.'

'No Yashi.' She shook her head, rattling her dangling earrings. 'This time we put the whole lorry on the boat. We are taking the passenger ferry!'

'No! We always send the container by rail!' He put his foot hard on the brake causing the rear tyres to squeal on the tarmac. 'Why you no tell me this?'

'Keep going, Yashi!' she continued as the driver was pulling to a stop.

'I am not going to England. I cannot go there. It stinks. Why you no tell me?'

'I said, keep going!' Yashi looked back over to her, seeing the barrel of a gun pointing right at him. 'Keep going, and keep calm. It will all be fine.'

The man looked nervous. He had never seen Alicia kill anyone but he didn't doubt for a second that she would if she had to. Slowly he pressed the throttle again and the lorry lurched forward, heading on towards the port.

'That's better. From now on, you do as I say. OK?' Yashi just nodded. 'Good. Now, head for the ferry terminal.' Within a few minutes, Alicia could see the big boat lined up alongside the harbour, with its pointed funnel black against the morning sunrise. As the lorry drew into the port, she got Yashi to pull over near the terminal building and jumped down from the cab.

'You come with me to get the tickets. Bring your passport.' Yashi climbed down from the cab, joining her on the tarmac, and she linked her arm through his. 'It will all be fine. You see?' she said, a little more soothingly. As they stepped through the double glass doors a man held them open for her and she flashed him a charming smile before making her way to the ticket office. Thankfully for her, a young man was serving and Alicia used that same smile on him, dazzling him with her eyes as he fumbled for the tickets. One lorry. Two passengers. Next sailing to Dover in 15 minutes.

'I need the men's room,' growled the Albanian once Alicia had the tickets in her hand.

'Well, don't be long!' She smiled at him again, watching him go and still unsure if she could trust him as she made her way to the ladies toilet. When she came out a few minutes later, she instantly knew something was wrong. Out on the tarmac, Yashi was running towards the lorry when a dark car pulled along side it and two men jumped out. One of them was huge and Alicia was sure she had seen him before. Her heart leapt into her mouth as she felt in her handbag for the revolver. This didn't look good. She had got so near and yet so far. Well, now was the time to stay cool. Just sit it out and watch through the window.

Within seconds, the larger of the two men had grabbed Yashi and wrestled him to the ground but Yashi was quick and he struggled free from the grasp. From then on, things got a bit confusing. As Yashi sprinted across the tarmac, the second man fired a shot which struck the ground just behind him.

'STOP! Or I will kill you!' shouted a man in a dark suit. 'You have been warned!'

Within a few seconds, two shots were fired, just as a police-car came screaming through the gates with its sirens blaring, hotly followed by a second one. The two cars circled the darker car which was still parked with its doors open.

'That's them!' shouted an English voice from the back seat of the second car. 'That's the Righteous Brothers!'

From then on there was a lot of shouting, some more shooting, and even a few punches thrown between all of the men. Alicia watched them concentrating on each other and on Yashi, as he fell to the ground.

Now, thought Alicia, now or never. As bold as brass, she stepped out through the doorway, strutted across the tarmac, pulled out a spare set of keys from her bag and climbed up into the lorry cab. Nobody took much notice as the lorry engine burst into life and drove off towards the car ferry, just in time to hear its loud foghorn sounding that they were ready to load. Alicia smiled to herself. Stupid men, always shouting and shooting each other. But then, as she glanced across to the passenger-side mirror, one of the stupid men to whom she was referring stared at her through the window, as he hung on to the mirror with both hands with a terrified grin on his face.

'Alicia!' mouthed the voice. 'Let me in!'

Alicia wasn't sure if it was out of pity or stupidity that she flipped the switch to lower the window, but when she had done, she could plainly hear the man shouting very loudly. If she could hear him, then so could other people.

'Shut up, you fool. Go away!'

But Try wasn't going away. This was the woman of his dreams and he wasn't going to let her go that easily. With almost superhuman strength, he hauled himself in through the open window of the moving lorry and bowled in on to the passengers seat.

'Alicia. Wait!' he said, pathetically.

'Shut up. And get down on the floor!' she hissed as they approached a small kiosk with a Union Jack flag on the side.

'Passport!' demanded the man and she immediately obliged by handing it to him. It seemed to take him ages to study it and then look at her face, before he broke into a half smile.

'Have a nice trip, Catherine,' he said, raising the barrier. Alicia flashed him a knowing smile and hit the throttle. As soon as they had moved on a bit further, Try's head popped up from below the seat.

'Catherine?' he asked, accusingly.

'It's a long story,' she smiled to him, as the wagon rattled over the metal ramp and into the dark cargo hold.

*

'Get your hands off my suit, you numpty frog-head,' snarled K, as Broule pulled his arm up behind his back. Serge wasn't being captured quite so easily, and was almost enjoying resisting arrest by swinging punches left and right. Eventually it took four police men to take him down and cuff him.

It was only when the two men were bundled into the back of a police van that Broule realised Try was missing. Oh well, he thought, at least we caught the villains.

Three minutes later he realised that they hadn't.

'You bloody stupid car chaser!' screamed his boss down the phone. While Broule was listening to what he had to say, he watched the huge car ferry sail out into the

English Channel and realised he had just made a very costly mistake.

Apparently, Serge and K weren't the men's real names at all, just a couple of alias's that they used when working undercover. Both men were actually members of the International Police Department, or Interpol as they were commonly known. Although the extent of the information given to Officer Broule, who was a mere traffic cop, was quite scarce, it seemed these two had been watching a couple who had been smuggling illegal immigrants across Europe. The man, known as Yashi, was wanted for at least two counts of murder but rather than bring him in, they had followed him, trying to reveal the complete operation in conjunction with the British Customs. Unfortunately, as Yashi had been killed trying to escape by one of the two men, their line of questioning was still non-existent.

Broule was to be held solely accountable for ruining 6 months of under-cover work by disturbing the men at their time of arrest, while allowing the other suspect, name unknown, to go free with the illegal cargo. What did he have to say for himself?

Well Broule did have something to say; a few things actually.

Why hadn't they pulled the lorry over sooner?

Why had these men interrogated and beaten senseless a seemingly innocent civilian, one Mister Trevor Hard?

Broule had some more information that may be useful to them if they would stop blaming him for everything.

At this point he requested that he be taken in for questioning for his own safety. Despite his superior officer advising him not to be so bloody stupid and that the only danger he was in was when the Super got hold of his balls, Broule protested that he needed sanctuary.

'You can speak in front of these men, they are International agents for fuck's sake!' he was told, but still he stood his ground.

Eventually, Broule was taken from the van and driven to the local police station. Meanwhile, when the two International agents were released, the one in the dark suit made a few phone calls, all to England.

'Right, this better be good!' said an irate senior officer who just driven all the way up from Paris. Seated in the sparse interview room, Broule cleared his throat. This one was by the book and he had to get it right.

'Interview commencing at 8.32 am, Calais Police station, Officer Ludovic Broule under oath...'

'Yes, yes. Get on with it, man!'

'When the man known as Yashi was running across the tarmac, he was warned that he must stop or be killed. The man did stop and turned round with his hands in the air. At that point, the agent known as Serge raised his gun and fired twice, killing him instantly!'

'Are you saying that the agent murdered him on purpose?' snapped the officer.

'I am only saying what I saw, Sir!' replied Broule, cautiously. 'There may be other witnesses.'

'And, what else. You said you had information for us.' Broule cleared his throat again.

'In a forest near Poitiers, we picked up a man who was suffering from amnesia. The man was English.'

'Go on!'

'He was badly beaten but eventually, the man started to recall names, firstly his own and then a few more names.' Broule went to stand up. 'May I, Sir?' The man nodded so Broule pulled out his notebook.

'The name he gave me was of a Max Hornsby. He wasn't quite sure what the connection was, but first the woman had asked him if he knew this name and then the two agents interrogated him about it.' Pausing for a few seconds, Broule continued. 'Sir...,' he cleared his throat, 'we also have another English man in custody!'

'Another one? Where?'

'In La Rochelle, Sir. Only...' Broule looked to the ground. 'Only he claims to be police officer too.' This time Broule had anticipated the reaction and sat still looking straight ahead as the senior officer shouted out a long list of expletives in French.

'What on earth do you think you are doing, going around arresting English Police Officers? Have you any idea what this will do for Anglo-French relations?'

'Our people in La Rochelle interrogated him at his bedside.'

'Bedside? Ye Gods, don't tell me you shot him?'

'No Sir. But someone hit him, pretty hard.'

'Will he live?'

'Yes, Sir. He'll pull through. I phoned to check a while ago.'

'Thank God!'

'I also gave the department a name to run by him, and he confirmed it.'

'Hornsby?'

'Yes, Sir?' said Broule quietly, when the man had finished ranting. 'Sir. I believe Max Hornsby is you main man, Sir. And I am under the opinion that these two agents may just be taking bribes from him!' There. He had said it now and it was on tape. Broule was a man who rarely acted on hunches these days, but when they came around, he was pretty sure he could trust them. Ludovic Broule was also a man who had seen far too much corruption in his time as a detective. Now he was sticking his neck on the line.

'Jesus Christ on a bike…!' said the senior officer. 'Did you hear what you just said?' Broule nodded. 'On what evidence do you make this claim?' Broule said nothing for a moment so the man repeated the question.

'On a hunch, Sir!' muttered Broule.

'A fucking hunch?! You're a fucking traffic cop.'

'Yes, Sir. But my hunches have never been wrong before….!'

*

'Alicia? Or Catherine, or…or…,' Try trailed off.

'You can call me Alicia, it's OK,' she sighed. 'How did I end up with this little man?' she thought.

'There's something I think you should know?' Try continued.

'Oh Christ, are you still declaring your undying love for me? I told you, we wouldn't be compatible!'

'No, it's not that. I've been thinking about things and…..'

'Yes?' Her smile nearly floored him, even in this dim light.

'I think…er!'

'Spit it out Mister Hard!'

'I th..think there is someone in the back of your lorry!' he stammered finally.

The way Alicia laughed reminded him of when he had first clapped eyes on her, only yesterday, and they had shared a joke about Madame Meatier. This time the laugh was deeper, more genuine, as her shoulders rose up and down uncontrollably and her earrings jangled. And then, quite unexpectedly, Alicia reached across the seat, cupped Try's face in both hands and kissed him.

'You really don't know, do you?' she whispered, smiling again.

Try didn't, but from that moment on, he didn't care!

*

'The cargo is travelling single-handed.'

'Single-handed?'

'It might require some assistance.'

Before the man on the other end of the line could respond, the agent known as K closed the phone, cutting him off.

'No longer our problem,' he said, turning to Serge before brushing a few specs of dust from his suit. 'Target taken care of and goods shipped out of our jurisdiction. Except we don't know about any goods, do we?'

'Job done then?' Serge grinned. 'Shame about the target, what wiv im getting accidentally killed like that. Maybe e'll think twice before he pulls the trigger on one of us again.' Serge broke into a laugh. 'But e can't anymore, can e!' The two continued to laugh as they headed towards their dark sedan.

*

'You get that phone number?' asked the Inspector in French as he watched the two men from the back of a white Ford van with blacked out windows. Before the technician could answer he turned to Broule. 'You'd better be right about this hunch or your sorry ass will be behind an empty desk counting paper-clips for the rest of your days!' Broule said nothing.

'Yeah, got it. The number is registered in Birmingham, England, to a Hornsby Enterprises.' Ludovic heaved a sigh of relief but still remained silent.

'Good. And you got a wire in that car?'

'Yep. Receiving loud and clear!'

'Well, record everything for the next 12 hours, OK?' The man nodded. 'I mean everything. I wanna know when they go for a piss and how many sugars in their coffee.' He turned to Broule. 'You!' he said sharply. Broule raised a weary eyebrow. 'You come with me to my office in Paris. Let's see if we can piece this thing together!'

12

Passenger ferries can be quite noisy things but it wasn't until the huge boat clanged against the dock that Try woke with a jolt. Rolling over in the narrow bunk bed, he opened his tired eyes to focus on the empty space beside him that, the last time he had looked, had been filled with a beautiful woman. For a minute he suspected that last night had all been a dream, as he ran his hand over the dented pillow where her head had laid.

'Alicia?' he called out loud but there was no reply. Outside the window lorry engines revved up, the noise echoing around the cargo deck as they warmed up their heaters and refilled air-brake tanks. Try sat up and bumped his head on the bed above him and then pushed it with his hand to see if Alicia was up on the top bunk. She wasn't.

'*She's gone pal!*' said a voice in his head which sounded like its usual sceptical self.

'*Where could she have gone? We're on a boat..!*' answered Logic who was now fully back on duty.

'*Done a runner if you ask me?*'

'*Probably gone to the toilet,*' said Bladder Control who was hoping to do the same thing quite soon.

Try glanced to the dashboard to see a white envelope with the word TREV written on the front.

'*Well she can't go far, can she? She's left her lorry behind.*'

'*Yeah, she'd better come back soon, the ramps are opening. And we don't know how to drive this thing, do we? Had enough trouble with that new bloomin car he just bought. Damn foreign rubbish.*'

'*I could have a go,*' said Co-ordination, bravely.

He pulled open the note and read it, ignoring his conscience having a discussion inside his head. At the bottom of the envelope was a small key. The note was signed with a kiss.

'*Too late!*' said Eyes, glancing up from the note to see half a dozen men close around them with machine guns.

'You in the lorry!' shouted a voice through a loud-hailer as a spotlight shone in through the front window. 'Step down from the vehicle with your hands in the air!'

'*We really, really need to go to the toilet!*' said Bladder Control when a man with black leather gloves opened the driver's side door and pointed a gun inside.

Try screwed the note up, complete with the key, and swallowed it.

'Did you get that, Memory?' he whispered.

'I th..think so,' said Memory, 'but I can only hold it for a few hours!'

'I know how you feel,' said Digestion.

'I am not sure I can hold it that long...!' shouted Bladder.

*

As soon as the ramp touched down, a pretty woman stepped on to dry land and strutted over towards the Customs kiosk carrying a single leather bag, her short skirt flashing a glimpse of garter-top above her thigh-length boots to the guard as she passed him. Inside the kiosk, a dark-skinned man looked closely at her as she flicked her blonde fringe away from her eyes.

'Remove your sunglasses please, Madam?' The woman duly obliged, raising the front of her straw boater hat and throwing in a bright smile for good measure. Around her neck hung a splendid diamond necklace that glistened in the midday sun which the Customs officer studied for a few seconds until he was distracted by a colleague in the next booth. When his head was turned, she swallowed nervously. At last he turned back to her and smiled as well.

'Have nice day, Maam!' he said, signalling her to step through the turnstile. The blonde smiled again, replaced her sunglasses and was gone.

*

Try had never worn handcuffs before and found them most uncomfortable. Part of his brain told him to complain about the way he had been treated since he was dragged from the lorry, but Try didn't think these men were the type of people to listen to complaints.

So far he had been searched for weapons, asked at least ten times where his identity was, as well as the whereabouts of one Marisa Zobrinsky. Each time Try just shrugged his shoulders. He didn't know the answer to either of these questions so, for once, decided to listen to his Logic and stay silent. Eventually the cuffs had been removed when he had been allowed to go to the toilet and then pushed into a small room with no windows and told to wait there. As the door was locked, Logic and Sceptic sarcastically reasoned that this was the only possible thing he could do, although Adventure had suggested that they break out and hide somewhere. As usual his plan was ill-thought out.

Marisa? So that was her real name? Try thought that Alicia sounded much better and that was the name he would always remember her by. Somehow, he didn't think he would ever see her again but he had the memory of last night, when she had kissed him and then laid her head on the pillow next to him all night. Try had just slept with, albeit fully clothed, the most beautiful woman in the world. Whatever happened to him now didn't matter anymore.

Out in the corridor he could hear the sounds of quite a few people talking in a foreign language, including some shouting and crying.

Earlier that day Alicia had told him a few things but she said it was best if he didn't know everything, that way he wouldn't have to lie to the police. She said that during her life she had done some bad things, but he was instantly ready to forgive her for those. What she was doing now, was helping other people achieve their dream and Try thought that was most commendable, despite it being illegal. She had admitted that there were voices in the back of the lorry and that they belonged to people who deserved a better chance in life. That was how she had left it, when she put her arm around him and kissed him goodnight. Try had whispered in her ear that he would never forget this night and then gone sound asleep. The fact that it was in actual fact mid-morning never occurred to him, as the lorry rocked quietly from side to side for a couple of hours in the darkness of the freight deck and he occasionally awoke to feel the warmth of her breath on his neck.

Now she was gone, and he was alone, he had chance to think through what had happened. Also, he recalled the note, trying his best to remember it, word for word by continually recalling from his memory, then reciting it silently to himself 3 times. Soon they would come and ask him questions and he would have to block it out so that nobody else would ever know what it said. Deep inside him, his stomach rumbled and he realised that a piece of paper and small key were the only thing he had eaten for hours.

In the next cell, a tagging process had begun, as each of the 12 weary travellers was identified and reams of paperwork completed. Each one would have a story, each one a name, and each one a problem they were running from. Try felt sorry for them all.

As is the law of International Politics, all 12 of the illegal immigrants were entitled to immunity from prosecution and would be held in an open prison until expulsion and extradition laws had been argued over in the high courts. Then, probably in a few months time, they would be deported back to their lowly peasant lives, despite having parted with all of their savings. When it was her turn, Mimosa just put her head in her hands and cried, tears spilling down on to the paper triplicate form on the desk before her, as the Customs officer read out her rights, first in English and then in Polish. Through the wall Try could hear her sadness which pushed its way through his thoughts.

'*You need to help her!*' said his Heart, whose strings were stretched to breaking point.

As a British citizen and a felon, Try had no such rights, except the right to remain silent, one which so far he had exercised. He also had rights to a have a lawyer present and if he didn't have one, one would be appointed for him. The only other right he had was to a phone call, but he couldn't really think of anyone to call. Yes there was Helen Cartwright, but he didn't want to bother her and he was pretty sure even she couldn't help him out of the mess he was in this time.

When the door was opened, the sound of sobbing intensified as an overweight man in an ill-fitting cheap suit pushed his way through and closed it behind him.

'Mister Hard,' he said smarmily, holding out his hand for Try to shake. 'Can I call you Trevor?'

'If you like.'

'Trevor, my name is Andrew Scrase. I have been appointed as your attorney for today so that maybe I can help get us out of this place.'

'Us?' asked Try.

'Yes, us! I like to think that we can be a team. You and me, tell our little secrets to each other and then we might have a single believable story.' Try considered this for a minute.

'OK. You start,' he said.

'Start what?'

'You tell me all your secrets and I'll see if I believe you.'

'Well, when I say our secrets, I mean your secrets. You don't want to know my secrets.'

'So you do have secrets, Mister Scrase. Let's start at the beginning.' The man looked confused.

'Why don't you tell me yours first,' he said eventually.

'I already told everything I know,' sighed Try, 'about 20 times!'

'Well, why don't you tell me, and I'll see if it sounds true, shall I?'

'No.'

'No?' The man stepped back.

'No, I won't tell them to you to see if they sound true, because they don't. But they are. So what's the point? You see, no-one ever believes Try Hard. No one ever considers the little guy might be innocent. They just laugh. And you will just laugh. So there's no point at all.' Try was recalling his days back at boarding school when masters and boys would try and beat the truth that they wanted to hear out of him. He knew how this went. Eventually they would advise him to tell some lies to try and save himself.

'Why don't I start with a few questions then,' said the overweight solicitor, wiping his brow with a red spotted handkerchief.

'If you like?'

'Mister Hard. You don't sound as though you want to get off this charge?'

'What happened to Trevor?'

'Alright. Trevor!'

'What charge?'

'Well, I am not sure yet. You haven't yet been charged with anything.'

'Good. Can I go now?'

'I am afraid it isn't that simple.'

'I am innocent.'

'Of what, Trevor. Innocent of what?'

'Everything!'

'Trevor, you were driving a lorry containing illegal immigrants into the British Isles, and you were caught red-handed.'

'I wasn't driving.'

'Well, who was?'

'I don't know!'

'You don't know who was driving the lorry that you were sitting in, which contained 12 illegal immigrants? Why ever not?'

'I was asleep.'

'Asleep? When?'

'All the whole time.'

'And what time would this be?' said the lawyer, becoming a little too smug.

'Don't let him trick you!' shouted Logic, wisely.

'He knows something,' said Feeble, cowering in the dark.

'No he doesn't. He's bluffing. Sound him out!' advised Sceptic.

'You tell me?' said Hard. Inside his head, just about every compartment was screaming out advice.

'Look Mister Hard....'

'Trevor!' said Try calmly. 'Or Try.'

'Try? Try what?'

'Try Hard.'

'What the blazes are you on about you stupid little man...!' this outburst cemented Sceptic's argument that this fat man was no help what so ever.

'*Told you,*' it said.

Andrew Scrase took a deep breath, trying to re-gather his professionalism. He had had a long night himself, baby-sitting for his new baby while his wife had been out drinking with her girlfriends, which should have been a simple task. But the child was teething and wouldn't stop screaming until eventually he had to phone his own mother at midnight to get some advice. And now he had this lunatic to defend, who was obviously as guilty as slug in a greengrocers. If it wasn't for the money, he would have stayed in bed this morning. Now he was wishing he had.

'Let's start again, shall we, Trevor?'

'OK. You first this time?'

And so the sequence began again until Andrew's half an hour was up, at which time he sat quietly and completed a form which he pulled out of his briefcase.

In the box where it asked if there were any exceptional circumstances to consider, he wrote: 'CLIENT IS DERANGED!' in red letters. Then he packed up, gave Try a courteous smile and left the room in search of coffee.

'*That didn't go well?*' said Optimism.

*

Max Hornsby slammed his fist down on the desk for the umpteenth time, making his computer screen flicker and all the ornaments jump in the air.

'I don't fucking care if they have all been arrested. The government will let them out, eventually, especially with a little persuasion. What I want to know is where is that fucking Polack woman. And who is this prick called Hard. I'll give him Hard!'

'We don't know, Sir!' said a rough looking man who had reported the news. 'She is nowhere to be found. It seems that he is disguised as an English tourist, but with Albanian connections!'

'Albanian? Those communist bastards?' Max stopped to think for a few seconds. 'You think it's them?' The other man raised his eyebrows as if to agree but not wanting to implement his opinion. 'You think they are out to screw me? Why would they do that?' Max thumped the desk again. 'Find out what he knows then kill him?' he shouted. 'And find that woman!!!'

Max sat back down to his desk as the employee left the office, his head in his hands, trying to think why the Albanians would double-cross him. Surely they wouldn't be so stupid as to send one of their men over with the cargo. Unless he was a plant? Was that it, would he spill the beans? Give evidence, maybe? Max was trying to recall who within the operation could connect his name to it. There would be no trace on the lorry, it was registered in Europe and they would never be able to connect him to that. Seemingly, the girl was gone, not that she would talk anyway. She was a tough one.

Or had she been the one to double-cross him? What was that she had said: a prisoner on board? But then she had said he had been dealt with. No, he didn't think it would be her.

The driver? He had been dealt with too, by his man on the inside in the International Police. No. All in all he reckoned he was clear.

*

'They'll get picked up at the other end, I guess?'

'Sure, but that's not our problem. Max has ways of dealing with Customs Officers.'

'And we get paid extra for putting down the Albanian?'

'Yep, an extra grand!'

'What about that Englishman?'

'Him? Ha.' Agent K laughed so loud that the line crackled. 'A minnow like him won't even show up on the radar. Before he talks, Hornsby's mob will soon have him silenced.'

Ludovic Broule winced when he heard this over the speaker and was just about to object when the Inspector raised a hand to silence him.

'It's not him that worries me. It's the girl. I think she knows too much,' continued the agent.

'You think we should track her down? Do her in?'

'Steady down, Batman. You've killed enough people today!' Then a car engine started up and the talking ceased.

*

'Sounds like this guy Hornsby has people on the inside of everything!' said the Inspector, stretching his neck muscles. 'If what they say is correct, your man Hard will be dead by morning!'

'Shouldn't we do something?'

'WE?' snapped the senior officer. 'What we do is pass on information back to the British. It's not our problem then, is it? But we need to be sure we can bag these two goons from Interpol. They are a fucking problem and they are our fucking problem!' The inspector reached for the telephone. 'Get me the British immigration police?' he yelled at whoever answered it. 'Vite!'

Broule wasn't quite so convinced that this was the right course of action. If this hood had corrupt people within the British Customs service, then calling the immigration police would be playing right into their hands.

'Shouldn't we try and catch the whole operation between us?' he asked, perhaps a little naively. 'If we alarm them that we're on to them, then they will all close ranks and we won't get anyone?' For a second the Inspector ignored him but then suddenly he put the receiver back down on its cradle.

'Since when did you become Chief Inspector?' he asked Broule, sarcastically. The man took a sip of coffee and sat down. 'I've seen your resume,' he said at last, 'caught up in a corruption racket.' Broule just stared towards the window. Whenever he did anything slightly out of his line of duty, his old record always came back to haunt him.

'I was never charged!' he sighed, looking towards the exit. The inspector said nothing, just sat pondering.

'I suppose you want to put the record straight? Is that it?'

'Something like that, yes. I've seen too much corruption in my time of service.' It was Broule's turn to be silent and think for a second or two. 'But if you want me to help, I would like to be involved.'

'But what about the motorists?' answered the Inspector, with more sarcasm. Broule refrained to comment. 'Alright,' sighed the senior officer eventually. 'I will speak to the Super and see what resources we have.'

'Thank you, Sir!' The man nodded towards the door and Broule upped to leave. Before he closed the door he spoke again. 'Sir?'

'Yes?'

'I think we should act fast, Sir. Maybe we can save the Englishman!'

*

In a warm and musty cell, Try was wishing someone would. After his meaningless interview with the lawyer, he had been left on his own for a while before two large black guards came and dragged him out of the room and down a corridor. As he half walked and half glided, they passed a large cell with sturdy bars across the front behind which sat half a dozen men of various ages, each with a dark complexion and a forlorn look of anxiety. Each one looked up expectantly as he passed. Try glanced at them, looking for one in particular but he didn't see her.

The rest of the cells were closed steel doors with just a peep-hole so that the guards could look in. After they had passed a couple, a door was opened and Try was thrown into the next one. It wasn't much, just a bed against one wall and a sluice in the corner for a toilet.

'There you go, Son, you get the honeymoon suite all to yourself?' chuckled one of the men as he locked the door behind him.

While he had been left alone, Try had considered his situation more carefully, mulling a few ideas around for discussion amongst his various brain divisions.

Although he was innocent, he had already realised that it didn't look that way. He also considered the fact that he probably did have some information that the authorities would be pleased to hear. Some of it he had told to the French gendarme when he was in the back of the police car, despite not much of it making sense at the time. For instance, he was pretty sure that someone called Max Hornsby was involved in this illegality. Perhaps he could use this information to help his cause. He also had some other information stored inside of him. And it was wanting to get out.

'Guard?' he called out. 'Is there anyone there?'

'Mister Bikes?' came back an answer from the next cell.

'Samosa?' he replied, surprised. 'Is that you? Are you alright?'

'Yes, I think so. It's Mimosa!'

'Well, hang on in there!'

'Hang?'

'Just stay cool!' he said, and immediately knew that didn't make sense either.

'I want to be cool. Is hot in here!'

'Mimosa?'

'Yes, Mr Bikes?'

'I can help you!'

*

Ludovic Broule manoeuvred his powerful motorbike into a parking space on the side of the lower car deck, pulling it up on its stand and then securing it with some canvas straps.

This wasn't the exact instruction he had been given, travelling to England on the next ferry. In fact, his instruction had been quite the opposite, telling him to stay put in Paris for now, until they had confirmation from his superior officers to bring him in on the case. But Broule had a feeling that, by then, it may be too late.

*

Sleep wasn't an easy thing to come by in a busy prison but Try was so exhausted that he heard very little through the night until he was awoken by his cell door being unlocked. Sitting up on his hard bed, he tried to focus his eyes through the dim light to see who was coming in, but the door never opened. Curiously he staggered to his feet and padded over to the heavy door in his socks and gave it a push. It opened then.

'Hello?' he said quietly, poking his head out into the stark corridor lit with dim orange lighting. When there was no sign of anyone, Try's mind started to race, as various compartments woke up from their deep slumber and clambered out on duty, some still metaphorically brushing their hair.

'*The door's open..*' said Opportunism with a yawn.

'*We can see that,*' said Logic, 'but why? *Why is it open?*'

'*It's open, because someone just unlocked it?*' said Sarcasm.

'*Let's go through it and find out,*' replied Opportunism, who was the only one who seemed fully awake. '*If it's open, we can walk out of here. I can't say I like being trapped in a prison cell. I want to be free.*'

'*Not so fast….!*'

'*Oh, I wondered where you where?*' said Sarcasm, sarcastically. '*Having a lie in were we?*'

'*As a matter of fact, I was just checking a few things,*' replied Sceptical.

'*Yeah, yeah, wotever!*' Sarcasm wasn't going to miss his chance to have a dig at one of his main rivals.

'*Come on you lot, let's go!*' shouted Opportunism, or Oppo as he was known to his friends.

'*Look. Something smells fishy here. So let's just wait a minute.*' Sceptical had now fully woken up. Senses had woken up too, but couldn't smell anything, except the toilet in the corner. '*A prison door doesn't just unlock itself and let prisoners out, does it?*'

'*It didn't unlock itself. Someone unlocked it,*' said Logic, using all his logic.

'*Precisely!*' Sceptical was shaking his head. '*Someone wants us to go through it.*'

'*Great. So let's go,*' said Oppo, trying to persuade Try to put his shoes on.

'*Sep has a good point there,*' said Logic. '*Why would someone let us out, in the middle of the night? It's illogical!*'

Try sat on the bed listening to his thoughts. Within a few more seconds, they all – except Oppo, who was tugging at his sleeve – came to the same conclusion at the same time.

'IT'S A TRAP!' he shouted.

'*Come on, let's get some more sleep. We can deal with this in the morning,*' yawned Logic's big brother, who was a prefect and had just come down to tell them off for talking after lights out. He put his arm around Oppo's shoulders. *'We will be much better at escaping when we've all had a good night's sleep, won't we?'* he said patronisingly.

Try closed his eyes again.

A few minutes later, he heard another voice that was most definitely not inside his head.

'Mister Bikes?' Ears heard it first and gave him a nudge.

'Mimosa?'

'You said you could help me?' it continued.

'Not now. Later!'

'But Mister Bikes, your door is open!'

'Yes, I know that, but I am asleep,' he whispered agitatedly.

'Oh.' The word Oh had a certain tone about it. After a few seconds Try replied.

'What do you mean, Oh!?'

'Well, when you said you could help me, I think you may be a hero or something? But if you a hero, why you not open the door and escape. Take me with you.'

Try thought about this, summoning up the posse once again.

'*See, I told you,*' said Oppo.

'*Hero?*' spluttered Cowardice. '*Who said we are a hero? I'm not a hero. What did you tell her we were a hero for? I'm not going out there, doing hero stuff. Last time we tried that, I got a severe headache!*'

'*We didn't tell her we were a hero, did we,*' said Sceptical, '*but we did offer to help. Or at least some of us did.*' He gave Cowardice the sort of glare that he thought a Sergeant Major might use while trying to get his platoon to go over the top.

'*Ask her if her door is unlocked as well?*' whispered Logic, hoping his big brother wouldn't hear him.

'*Of course it's not unlocked. Because if it was she would have opened it and escaped, wouldn't she?*'

'Not necessarily,' argued Logic. '*We didn't, did we? Go on, ask her?*'

'Is your door unlocked as well?' whispered Try obediently, and then waited patiently for an answer.

'No. If it unlocked, I would opened it and escaped, wouldn't I?' said Mimosa, in the same tone she had used when she had said 'Oh' earlier.

'*See. Told ya.*' Smugness was not one of Logic's better attributes.

'*Hmmm!*' said Sceptical. '*What we have here is a conundrum?*'

'*A what?*' Cowardice wasn't the most literate member of the crew.

'*A conundrum,*' whispered Logic. '*Where there are a few different choices we can make which all seem similar, but we need to make the right one in order to reach the correct end. Like a puzzle, sort of thing.*'

'*Oh good. I like puzzles,*' replied Cowardice, a little more settled now. '*Except snakes and ladders. I am always worried the snakes might bite.*' Sceptical ignored him.

'*On the one hand, it may be a trap. But on the other hand, if we don't escape and save the lady, she wont think very highly of us, will she? Now personally, I am not too bothered what the lady thinks, but there may be other factions among us that think otherwise. Talking of which, where is Libido. He was all up for playing around this morning, dirty little beggar. Give him a shout someone? He's probably sleeping off that kiss from earlier.*'

'*Maybe we should take a vote on it? Democratically?*' reasoned Logic who was never comfortable making decisions on his own.

'*Demo-cratic-ly?*' asked Cowardice.

'It means that we all have a say. One cell, one vote. Like American's do.'

'Oooh! I'm not sure I like the sound of that. You mean, like Cowboys and Indians and MacDonalds and things?'

Logic let out a big sigh.

'Look. We are pretty sure what your vote will be, Cowie. Just Trust me, OK? When I nudge you, you stick up your hand!'

A vote was taken, democratically, and a decision reached. Wearily Try pulled on his shoes and smoothed down his sticking up hair, before pushing the door wide and heroically stepping out into the corridor.

13

Clutching her fashionable Louis Vuiton bag on her lap, Alicia sat quietly on the busy underground train full of London's commuters, avoiding the stare from a lecherous businessman in a long brown mac. She smiled to herself. They would be out looking for her, she knew that. Hornsby had men everywhere, especially in places of authority. But she hadn't harmed him, not really? As long as she kept silent and didn't go to the police he would forget her eventually. And she wasn't about to go to the police, not with what she was carrying in her bag. Absentmindedly she ran her fingers over the barrel of the handgun in her pocket, comforted by its security. Where she was going wasn't the safest place in town and she couldn't afford to get jumped. Above her, another man in a suit was bunched up close to her seat and she realised that he was probably looking down the front of her low cut jumper. How could these people endure this rat-race every day? It was inhumane. Without saying anything, she squashed the sharp end of her stiletto into his toe and he jumped back. Two more stops and she could breathe a bit easier.

*

Broule wasn't breathing any easier as he waited impatiently while the ramp was lowered, creaking on its hinges temporarily rusted with sea water. Long before any of the cars started unloading, he had started his engine and revved it a few times, chucking out a cloud of white smoke as its cylinders un-choked themselves ready for action. Beyond the ramp lay a country he had never been to, unveiling in front of him as a band of daylight nudged its way over the horizon of stark chalk rock. Like a noble French knight, he nervously he bit into his lip, slipping his steed into gear and hoping he wouldn't be too late. In front of him the car finally pulled away and he dropped his visor ready to charge.

A guard in a peaked cap at Passport Control didn't question him as he flashed his gendarme badge under the light of the kiosk window and Broule almost felt like asking him which direction it was to the building that they used to detain immigrants, but then thought better of it. Surprise was his best weapon, although thankfully not his only one. Following the line of traffic out over the ramp, he had a good view of the floodlit dock, where queues of lorries were lined up, waiting for their early morning passage onto the European mainland. Up ahead the road parted into two lanes, a red overhead sign saying Goods to Declare next to a green one: Nothing to Declare. He chose the green lane and coasted the bike quietly through a low slung archway expecting to see lines of menacing looking Customs Officers and sniffer dogs behind long tables but, to his surprise, there was no one, just a camera overhead, blinking a red light to tell him he was on film. 'Max has his ways of dealing with Customs Officers!' That was what the agent had said. Ludovic guessed that they would be tapping into the camera whenever they wanted. Nowadays, that sort of thing was easy. Better not pull the bike over here or someone would soon turn up. Glancing around, he looked for what might serve as a probable building where they would hold people who had broken the rules, but nothing looked likely so he continued out into the rising daylight and found a car park.

This time he pulled out his small field glasses and took a better look around the place. To the right, tight under Dover's chalk cliffs were some more buildings marked simply with Her Majesty's Crown. These ones had no windows, just one central doorway lit by a number of bright lights. If he wandered in through there he would surely be seen. Would a French Gendarme be welcomed in a British Customs house? It wasn't a risk he was prepared to make and he scanned around for another access. Behind a high chain-link fence, there were a number of Police cars, marked in familiar blue and orange. That would be the main station, probably containing a number of cells. Broule was pretty sure that was where he needed to be as he placed the glasses back in his pocket and fired up the engine again.

*

Out in the dim corridor, Try checked the door to the next cell which was secure, and then pulled back a small sliding hatch and looked inside. Behind the hatch a face peered back at him, wearing a head-shawl and square glasses. When she smiled, her front teeth were crooked.

'Mister Bikes. You came for me?' Try smiled back but then his face turned more serious. 'I don't have a key,' he whispered. Mimosa's face saddened. 'But...but, I will see if I can find one!'

With that he closed the hatch and tiptoed along the corridor. At the far end he was surprised at the lack of security in this place, as yet another door was left unlocked. With his brain shouting out conflicting instructions, he pushed the door gently and peered around it into a dark room. As far as he could tell, there was nobody in this room either; the whole place was like the Marie Celeste on a quiet day. Another corridor led from this room and Try could see daylight starting to seep in from a glass door at the far end. That would surely be an escape route? Now his conscience started to call out an argument.

'*What about the girl?*' said the more heroic voices.

'*Sod the girl, let's get outta here!*' answered the voice of reason, which was the slightly louder side of the house.

'*Here! Here!*' echoed a collaborative vote, and with that Try pushed the door open and headed along the corridor towards daylight and freedom. Suddenly, a row of fluorescent tubes of light flickered on above him, bathing the long walkway in light so bright that Try could see finger-mark stains on its once white walls.

'*Stop!*' screamed a cacophony of voices in his head.

'Going somewhere, Mister Hard?' called out a real voice, behind him. Try turned to face the voice, which belonged to a slightly built security guard with a pencil moustache. 'Tut, tut, Mister Hard!' it continued, the voice almost theatrical. 'Trying to escape, are we?' Try said nothing, just looked at the man and then towards the glass-door 3 metres away in the other direction.

'*You could make it,*' suggested Optimism inside his head, but that was met with a barrage of denial. As if reading his thoughts – which would be a magnificent feat for even the cleverest of psychiatric mind-readers – the security guard made a suggestion for him.

'Go ahead, Mister Hard. Make my day!' A couple of the compartments in his head had a brief argument about whether it was a line from an Arnold Schwarzenegger film, or one by Clint Eastwood, while the rest of them recognised the real danger when they saw the gun that the man was holding. 'You may as well run for it Mister Hard, or should I call you Try? Go on Try, Try! Try hard to get away. Because I have a job to do here, Try, a very important job.' The man sniggered to himself for a few seconds. 'I like my job, Try, because it means I get to carry out orders. And I like to obey orders, that's why I was in the Army.' The man pulled out a cigarette with one hand, put it in his mouth and lit it casually, blowing smoke out towards the ceiling. 'Well, Try, today I have a very special order, directly from the boss himself. He phoned me up personally. 'Spaz' he said.' Spaz grinned. 'Did you hear that, he called me by my nickname? The boss himself. 'Yes, Max?' I replied. He didn't like it when I called him by his first name though. 'It's Mister Hornsby to you, Son,' he said.' Spaz blew out a smoke ring. 'Now listen Spaz,' he says. 'I have a very special order for you today. You have to stop prisoners when they escape, don't you Spaz? Maybe they might try to run and your job is to stop them, isn't it Spaz?' That's what he told me. 'It would be quite unfortunate if one got shot trying to escape?' His very words.'

Try was listening to this, and decided it didn't sound good.

'I...I was going for a walk!'

'Sure you were!'

'My door was open, so I thought I would take some air..!'

'Your door? Oh now it wasn't open, was it? I checked it myself and I am sure it was locked. Reckon you may have picked the lock, perhaps?'

'Picked the lock? What with?'

'Oo, I dunno,' he drew in a long breath. 'Maybe a piece of wire or something? After all, you are an international criminal, Mister Hard. I am sure a man of your means would do something like that.' Spaz stubbed his cigarette out under the heel of his boot. 'So go on then. Off you go!'

Try turned to look at the door again. It was only a few metres but if this guard was army trained, he wouldn't stand a chance. It would be like shooting ducks in a barrel. Really stupid ducks, that had climbed in to hide from a hunter and then quacked very loudly.

'Well, what are you waiting for?'

Try stayed put.

'Well, technically you are already escaping I suppose, because you are outside your cell and heading for the door. I will have to stop you.' Try glanced up above his head to see a security camera pointing down towards the doorway and Spaz followed his gaze. 'What, that? Don't worry about that thing, I'll soon get the tapes.'

'What if we went back inside?' suggested Logic. Try repeated the question out loud.

'Ooh, you can't do that.' Spaz shook his head. 'If you come towards me, it will be self defence, see. And I am pretty good at doing self defence. Done it loads of times.'

'*He has a good point there,*' agreed Sceptical. '*I reckon we are tatered!*'

'*Tatered?*' questioned Logic.

'*Yep. You know, like 'the game's up!' or 'up shit creek without a canoe!*'

'Oh. Well why didn't you say so. This is the end then, is it?'

'Noooo!!!!' screamed Cowardice dramatically.

'Hang on, what was that?' said Opportunism.

'Wha..! Ha, you nearly had me then, Oppo. I nearly fell for that old trick. Ha. The oldest one in the book!' Logic was starting to laugh in the face of Adversity, who had also just showed up.

'No. I'm serious. Look there it is again. Something moving outside the window!'

'Where?' said Sceptical. 'I don't see….Oh yes. It looks like a..'

'GET DOWN!' shouted Health and Safety. 'NOW!'

Frightened by this outburst, Try dived to the ground, just as the door burst open and a shot was fired which missed his brain by inches – which was just as well, as there were so many voices in his head that if it had been hit it would've been classed as mass genocide!

Spaz dropped to the ground, clutching his thigh, but still gripping the pistol which he pointed back down the corridor as a large man in a distinctive blue uniform ran towards him, leaping over Try where he lay.

'I've always wanted to say this,' said Oppo.

'Say what?' questioned Logic.

'Get the fuck outta here!' he screamed. Clambering on to all fours, Try scurried towards the outside doorway as another shot fired behind him. This time there was a yell and a loud crash as Broule landed on top of Spaz, sending him backwards through the doorway into the darkened room.

'Merd!' yelled Broule, as the guard slammed the door on his face, breaking a pane of glass. As Spaz tried to run, Broule caught him round the ankle, fetching him down to the ground again, but Spaz kicked out and caught the Frenchman under the chin.

'You want to play rough, do you, Johnny Foreigner. Well, I'll show you rough!' Spaz swung the butt of the pistol hard on Broule's skull, sending blood splashing out on to the wall. 'Now sit down, and let me do my job!' With that, Spaz jumped to his feet and then, hopping on one leg, chased after Try who had reached the outer door and was running out on to the tarmac.

'Prisoner trying to escape! Stop!' he muttered through gritted teeth, aiming the pistol at Try's back.

Just as he was about to fire, a bullet burst through his shoulder. 'How many times do I have to save this man's life?' thought Broule as Spaz buckled to the floor. But still he wasn't finished and turned his pistol towards Broule. This time the Frenchman had no choice but to put a bullet into his forehead!

'C'est Ca!' he said quietly to himself, which in English can mean anything between, 'Well done chaps, jolly good show!' and 'Oh fuck, I've really gone and done it now!'

After checking that the security guard was dead, Officer Ludovic Broule, former and possibly reinstated detective, recently demoted, went to the security room, located the correct machine and removed the tape, putting it small plastic bag. Then he went outside, hid the bag well out of sight under a concrete step and sat in the early morning light, watching Try running for his life into the distance. It wasn't long before the sky and the air were filled with the sounds of blues and two's heading his way.

*

'These are some very fine stones indeed!' said a little man with a pointy grey beard excitedly, as he peered at one diamond after another through a magnifying glass.

'I know,' replied the blonde. 'I am told you pay the highest prices?'

'Oh fey, I can give you good money, if you want to sell. But where did you get them? They are antiques!'

'They were my Grandmother's and I want to sell,' she said calmly. 'All but one of them.' She bent over the man, showing a little too much cleavage and selected a small object from amongst the table full of jewellery, which she wrapped in tissue paper and pushed into her purse. 'And you want to buy, so let's talk figures?'

When they had finished talking figures, Alicia stared down at the bankers draft as the little man wrote it, desperately trying not grin. She had never seen so many noughts outside of a South American telephone directory. Not a bad reward for few years of searching in the closets of some of Communism's most powerful tyrants when they were distracted. It hadn't been stealing, just redistributing some of the wealth that had been confiscated, only this time in her direction.

After shaking the little man's hand, she took a taxi and checked into the Sheridan Hotel in Mayfair, smiling at the nice desk clerk so that he upgraded her to the best room available. Once inside her room, after a refreshing shower, she pulled on yet another wig, this one dark auburn in colour in the shape of a fashionable bob. Adding finishing touches with some blushing make-up and lipstick, she made her way on foot to Coutts Bank on the Strand. At the reception she asked for the manager, producing a passport in the name of Ava Brinsky on which the photograph exactly matched her appearance, and deposited the cheque into a Swiss bank account under the same name.

As she stepped outside into the busy London traffic, a handsome man smiled at her from the front seat of a red Ferrari as he waited for the traffic lights to change. Alicia flashed him a smile back.

'You going my way?' she asked.

*

After a day in intensive care and two more days in an isolated ward in a French hospital, guarded round-the-clock by 2 gendarmes and the most fearsome Matron he had ever encountered, Baxter Collins was released without charge. Well, there was a charge, of just short of 400 euros for his treatment and board and lodgings.

'Haven't you ever heard of the National Health,' he mumbled, paying the woman at front desk and waiting 20 minutes for her to produce the correct paperwork, in triplicate, as his receipt.

'What do you mean, you lost him?' said the Superintendant on the other end of the phone. 'He's here, you blithering idiot!'

'Here, Sir?'

'Yes, here in England. Don't you watch the television, Man?'

'Er, sorry Sir. I have been otherwise detained.'

'Well. Get your sorry arse back to this office, pronto, so that I can boot it with my size 10 brogues!'

'Yes, Sir.'

'And Collins?'

'Yes, Sir.'

'Get that bloody car back here, too. My wife's going crazy since hers is in the garage for repairs again.'

'Yes, Sir,' sighed Baxter.

*

The arrest of Max Hornsby on charges of fraud and smuggling was indeed on the National news. Now the well known Mobster was in a police cell where his lawyers were doing their best to invalidate, destroy or blatantly lie their way out of any evidence put before them.

Try knew about police cells. Once he had been recaptured, that was where he had spent the last two days, except for when he was in the interview room – which was quite frequently.

A combination of Customs Officers, Immigration Police, Fraud Squad and Special Branch took it in turns to ask him baffling questions about Eastern Europe, Albania in particular, as well as a barrage of accusations about his involvement with Max Hornsby. Along with his appointed lawyer, Try's brain compartments took it in turns to offer him council with increasingly confusing results. In the finish, after a lot of head scratching and validation of his story by a French police officer, it was decided that the only charge they could pin on Trevor Richard Yashati Hard was that of entering the country without a passport and, in view of the fact that at least he did have one registered in his name in the UK, unlike the other 12 immigrants that they had locked up, it wasn't a charge worth pressing.

However, the case against Max Hornsby was rather a different matter and one that definitely was worth pressing. Over the last 6 months a variety of evidence had been gathered against him but none as strong as that which could be provided but one of their key witnesses, one Trevor Richard Yashati Hard.

For this reason, within minutes of being released without charge, Try was once again held in custody, this time for his own safety. It wasn't a pleasant thought.

'*Where is this safe-house*?' asked Logic.

'*We don't know that do we? If we knew where it was, then it wouldn't be that safe would it?*' said Sceptical with a little help from Sarcasm.

'*Well, someone must know where it is?*'

'*What does it matter where it is? As long as it's safe!*' said Cowardice.

'*What is a safe house?*' asked Inquisitive, who had only just been elected to the Brain's Trust and had a lot of catching up to do.

'*Never mind about the safe-house. What about the girl?*' said Libido, who had been snoozing for a couple of days.

'*Oh yes,*' said Logic, '*I had forgotten about her.*'

'*What about her?*' said Sceptical.

'*Well, she was rather nice. And we did promise we would help her.*'

'*How are we going to do that?*'

'*Wasn't there something about her in that note that the woman left?*'

'*Bloody hell! So there was!*' said Logic. '*Memory, can you come up here please? And can somebody ask where the toilet is?*'

*

'Whadda you mean, under arrest. You can't arrest me, I am a police officer!' growled Serge, looking around the crowded police station.

'Not any more, you're not. Hand over your badge please!' said the arresting officer, firmly.

'Just like that, eh?'

'We already have your partner in custody. He has told us everything.'

'Well, you aint got me, ave ya?' The big man flexed his knuckles.

'We can do this the easy way, or the hard way!' Another officer joined his side, and then another. 'But my guess is that you will prefer the hard way?'

With one last throw of the dice, Serge leapt into action, swinging both his fists like a madman. It was a fight that lasted for nearly 20 minutes as, one by one, most of the officers in the International police station in Antwerp joined in, all trying to get a punch or kick into this cheating corrupted man who had given the whole force a bad reputation. Eventually, when the man was nearly unconscious and a considerable amount of furniture destroyed, Serge was dragged down to the cells and locked up awaiting trial. Once he was gone, the Chief Superintendant opened the blinds to his office once more.

'A bit of a scuffle was there lads?' he asked innocently, opening his door and viewing the carnage and a few spots of blood about the place.

'Suspect resisted arrest, Sir! All in hand now.'

*

'I would like to see one to the immigrants please?' asked Try at the reception desk.

'No can do!' replied the clerk.

'But it's urgent!'

'Is it now? Well, why is that?' Try bit his lip, he couldn't divulge the real reason.

'Go on, play your trump card!' said Sceptical inside his head. 'Remember why you're still here?'

'Oh, Yes.'

'Yes what?' said the desk clerk questioningly.

'Um. As you know, I am to be a witness in a certain high profile trial,' announced Try confidently, after some more encouragement. 'And I would like to check some details with one of the people who were in the back of that lorry!'

'Oh. I see. Er. Yes. I suppose that could be allowed.'

Try followed the woman down the corridor to the cell door, sweat rising on the palms of his hands.

'Make it quick!' she snapped, almost pushing him inside and locking it behind him.

In the dim light, Try blinked, adjusting his eyes as the woman climbed up from the bed.

'Mister Bikes?' she said, with astonishment. 'You came back?'

'Samosa?' he said, looking at her for the first time.

'Mimosa!' she corrected him. Try studied her pretty face, lined with worry. The long robes and scarf she had been wearing when he saw her last had been replaced with a knitted jumper and flowery skirt making her look 15 years younger. Her feet were bare, but then Try guessed she would be used to that.

'Mimosa. I would like to help you, but it seems there is only one way that I can...'

'*The key! The Key!*' shouted a chorus in his head. Try put his hand in his pocket and pulled out the small key that had spent two days passing, sometimes painfully, through his internal digestive system. Holding it shakily in the palm of his hand, Try proffered it towards her. The Polish woman looked down at it, somewhat confused, but before she could speak, he continued with the lines that he had been given by Memory a few minutes earlier.

'They are intending to send you back to Poland, where you will go to jail. There is only one way I can help to save you from that.' Now Mimosa was not wearing her glasses he saw what lovely eyes she had and it put him off for a second or two. The voices gave him a kick. 'Locker number 2622, Paddington Station, London....' Try continued after clearing his throat, 'contains a diamond ring, that once belonged to Countess Barr..Bra...'

'Countess Bra?' she repeated, wondering what on earth was going on.

'*Countess Brinsky of Saltenpepp!*' hissed Libido, spurring him on.

'Countess Brinsky of Salt and Pepper,' continued Try as his face turned through orange to red faster than a New York traffic light. 'It was her engagement ring. And I was supposed to fetch it today, only I cannot go because I now have to stay inside on a heroic mission.'

'*I wrote that bit..*' said Cowardice, proudly. Try stalled then, taking a deep breath.

'*Go on!!*' shouted the council of voices.

'Mimosa?' he dropped to one knee, feeling the cold concrete against his knee cap. 'Will you marry me?'

THE END

Coming soon…..

It must be Hard

….. Due out May 2012

Settling into married life is never going to be easy for a confirmed bachelor….especially in a house with a garden.

There's the grass to contend with, to start with. Should grass really be 6 feet high. And why has Mavis got a loaf of bread on her head?

More hilarious capers with Trevor Hard.

Published by Chauffour Books

www.chauffourbooks.co.uk

Made in the USA
Charleston, SC
24 May 2012